Reflections
From
Jackie's World

JACQUALINE K. BOOG

WESTBOW
PRESS®
A DIVISION OF THOMAS NELSON
& ZONDERVAN

WestBow Press books may be ordered through booksellers or by contacting:

WestBow Press
A Division of Thomas Nelson & Zondervan
1663 Liberty Drive
Bloomington, IN 47403
www.westbowpress.com
844-714-3454

Interior Image Credit: Larry Boog

Scripture taken from the New King James Version® Copyright © 1982 by Thomas Nelson. Used by permission. All rights reserved.

ISBN: 978-1-6642-2266-3 (sc)
ISBN: 978-1-6642-2265-6 (e)

Print information available on the last page.

WestBow Press rev. date: 03/30/2021

ONE NIGHT WHILE MY GRANDDAUGHTER ARIEL WAS HERE FROM ARIZONA, I HAD the privilege of tucking her in for the night. She wanted me to snuggle with her so I crawled in bed beside her and just as we got comfy the phone rang. I had to answer it, so I left her for just a minute. When I got back she was out like a light. Apparently the time change and all the fun activity had finally caught up with her. So I left her to her well deserved sleep. But before I did, I got back in bed with her, gently wrapped my arms around her, stroked her hair and whispered in her ear, "I love you Ariel!" Tonight as I was remembering this, I thought about how often I fall into bed weary from a long day, almost dreading the next. But I was comforted by the thought that maybe, just as I am falling asleep each night, the Lord quietly comes near, gently strokes my hair, and whispers in my ear, "I love you my child!" I don't have to ask, He just comes. Because He understands, He knows, and He cares. And His gentle touch is sufficient to see me through each and every day! All the time, every time, just in time! Rest in Him tonight my friends. For He is always near and His love never fails!!

*I*WAS SHOPPING YESTERDAY AND NEEDED SOME PLASTIC SPOONS. AS I TOOK THEM off the counter the bottom of the box fell out and all 48 of them fell to the floor. I froze in place for a minute wondering if anybody had noticed. But the clatter of plastic spoons hitting a cement floor was hard to ignore. Then I considered just quietly walking away, but my conscious got the best of me and I knelt down to start picking them up. Most people looked the other way, oblivious to my plight except for one person. Over my shoulder I heard the words, "We will help." Three simple words. I turned and saw a young mother with her two small children coming to my rescue. They got down on the floor beside me and helped pick up spoons. And I thought, there are still people in this world who are willing to help someone in need, no matter how small, and they are teaching their children to do the same. And somehow that made me feel better about life in general. So, if you see someone who needs a helping hand, don't hesitate to reach out. Even if it's as simple as helping someone pick up spoons. Wait a minute, isn't there a game called "Pick up Spoons"? Or am I thinking about "spooning"? Ah.......never mind. That's an entirely different subject!! ☺ Point is....... make someone's day brighter. Help carry their load. Do what you can to ease the discomfort of another. Let's all pick up a few fallen spoons!

Jacqualine K. Boog

*I*WOULD LIKE TO EXPRESS MY PERSONAL DISAPPOINTMENT IN THE PERSON THAT decided an electronic toilet has the intelligence to decide when I have left the "seat"! While waiting for the ferry to Mackinaw Island, I decided I had better "go" before it was time to go. So, I found a stall, properly sanitized the seat (as all good ladies know how to do) and sat down. At which point I realized the door had not latched and was starting to swing open. So I leaned forward to push it shut and.......the toilet flushed! There is no way to actually describe what kind of feeling that is. I mean is it flushing? Is it spraying? Am I being sucked in or blown off? I abruptly sat back down without, unfortunately, latching the door! So I tried again, barely leaving the seat, and before I knew it....you guessed it....the second unnecessary flush! Now I'm really getting annoyed with this silly toilet and I believe I may have said so out loud! So I settled myself on the seat one more time, did what I came in to do, and just before I'm ready........ FLUSH NUMBER THREE!!! At this point I felt like I needed a shower or at least a change of clothes because I am now convinced the entire stall is filled with micro-droplets of some sort and I seriously don't even want to breathe! I will never trust one of these contraptions again! And if forced to use one, I will come prepared with extra weight in an effort to make it think...I'M STILL THERE!!!!!

*M*Y CO-WORKERS AND I WERE DISCUSSING THE OLD MOOD RINGS THAT WERE popular back in the 70's. The ones that turned different colors according to your "mood". And we were thinking how nice it would be if we had shirts that did the same thing so we would know who to stay away from. Like if someone came in wearing a shirt turning an angry fiery red, we'd be like....back away!! But if we saw someone who's shirt was turning a nice calm, soothing blue, we'd be following that person around all day. And then I realized we all have a "mood indicator". It's called our heart and it displays our mood on our face. Is your face smiling and comforting inviting people to seek you out? Or is it all scrunched up with a grumpy look making people "back away"! So, as we think about what our mood is, let's guard our hearts from the things that bring us down and tend to show up on our faces. Let's allow a little more joy and peace to radiate through our hearts and brighten up our faces. Let's do a little less frowning and a little more "feeling groovy"! Oops! Just slipped into a 70's mood! Can I get a "right on"?? How 'bout a "far out, dude"? The younger ones reading this just went....huh?? But my generation just said, "Cool!" and took a walk down memory lane!

WE HAVE AN ENCLOSED FRONT PORCH AND I WAS SITTING IN THE LIVING ROOM this morning when I realized there was a bird flying around out there. I sent my husband out to do something about it because - duh - isn't that what husbands are for?? He went out and opened the porch door in an effort to help the bird find its way out. A few minutes later he came in requesting my help. And I quote, "I want you to stand by the door and keep it from flying to the other end of the porch." Um….NO!! Like I want to be a human shield between a bird and its flight destination! Next thing I see out there is Larry walking back and forth with a red child-sized snow shovel being held high in the air. (Which I'm sure was providing a great source of entertainment for our neighbors!) Apparently he was trying to help it make its way toward the open door. Eventually he was successful, but I had to ask, "Did you smack that poor bird through the door with the shovel??" His answer, "Well…ah…I sort of "gently nudged" it out." Ya, right! I think that bird went flying off our porch like Angry Bird being flung from a slingshot!! But, here's the thing. I think we're all a little like that bird. We run back and forth trying to figure out which way to go when God has put the "open door" right there before us. Might I suggest the next time you're in that situation that you go ahead and step through that door before you are "gently nudged" (or flung) through it! I think once you are on the other side you'll find you're exactly where you're supposed to be!!

WE DID A LITTLE BABYSITTING THIS LAST WEEKEND AND OUR GRANDDAUGHTER Lily has become quite the explorer. She's crawling and climbing and wanting to see everything that's going on around her, including Nana's necklace, Papa's feet and a variety of other things within her reach. She somehow managed, under Nana's watchful eye, to get hold of some sparkly tissue paper which went directly into her mouth. I got most of it away from her but did warn my son that she might poop sparkles! (Which is befitting for a princess anyway!) She finally started winding down a bit and then got just a little cranky. So I picked her up, snuggled her up close to me, and began to rock her gently back and forth. She wanted nothing to do with that! She squirmed, she fought, she wiggled but eventually gave up the battle and rested in Nana's loving arms. How many times do we fight this same battle? How often are we afraid we'll miss something if we stop and rest for awhile? How many times have we squirmed out of the very resting place God has provided? So are you weary and worn? Go ahead and snuggle up close to your Savior. Let His loving arms hold you tight and be your place of rest. It may only be for a short power nap, but I guarantee it will refresh your soul. It worked for Lily!!

WE WENT TO SEE LILY BEAN SATURDAY NIGHT AND HER DADDY WANTED US TO see how fast she could crawl. He said, "Stay there and let her come to you." So we stood there and waited and Lily looked at me and then at Papa and then back to me and didn't budge! And her Momma said, "Um….. you've got to make her think you WANT her!" (Read that in a southern accent. It has way more effect!) Now I'm all over this. I get down on the floor, I clap my hands, I call her name…..nothing! Until her Daddy came and stood next to me (that little girl is all about her Daddy!) Now she's going lickity-split across the floor and right into my arms ready for hugs from Grandma. Coincidently, at the end of our Sunday morning service, Pastor Mike made a comment much like what Lily's Momma had said. "He wants to know you need Him!" Just like Lily needed to know she was welcome in my arms, so the Lord needs to know He's welcome in our hearts. And I can't help but think about the baby who came into the world so long ago, destined to be a King. He was like any other baby. He needed to know He was wanted. He needed to know He was cared for. He needed to know He was loved. And now as the King of Kings He still needs the answers to the same questions. And so He asks, "Do you need me? Do you want me? Do you love Me?" So, as you think about these things this Christmas ask yourself the same questions. Do you need Him? Do you want Him? Do you love Him? Go ahead. Open your heart to give Him all of you so you can have all of Him! And as you run lickity-split towards Him, be ready to receive abundant love!!

WE HAD A LOVELY CHRISTMAS DINNER WITH OUR SON MATTHEW AND HIS WIFE Jennifer and, of course, Lily Bean. We met at a lovely restaurant, where Jennifer works, for their buffet. Matthew brought Lily (Jen was already there) and she was absolutely adorable. He had her all dressed up in a beautiful red Christmas dress with a big bow and a little black jacket. Just too cute! We were enjoying our time together when Jennifer looked at Lily, her eyes kind of popped a little, and she began to smile. Matthew said, "What?" Jennifer said, "Nothing." He said, "What?" again. She just smiled. And then Matthew said, "Wait…is her dress on backwards? Seriously? I put Lily's dress on backwards!!" After thorough inspection it was quite clear that her dress was, in fact, on backwards!! Buttons and bow in the front that should have been in the back! We all laughed about it because honestly no one had really noticed. So I gave Matthew a high five! You know why? Because several years ago he was making all kinds of very bad decisions in his life. But today, in this moment, the worst decision he made was figuring out which was the back and which was the front of his daughter's Christmas dress! And I applaud his efforts! I applaud the way he has turned his life around. And I applaud the fact that he was more concerned that his little girl was dressed up pretty for Christmas than the fact that her dress was on backwards! And that, friends, is my Christmas story!!!

ONE OF OUR WORSHIP TEAM MEMBERS NEEDED AN EXTRA CHAIR AND I WAS helping him find one. We went to the storage room. You know the one. Every residence, business, and apparently churches have one. It's the room down the hall, past the chapel, next to the prayer room. (Like, where else would it be?) It contains all the items that once were, could have been, or hope to be in the sanctuary! As we left the room I stumbled over something. I turned and looked to find.......I had stumbled over the manger! The very representation of our Savior's humble birth! And it's half my size! Kind of hard to miss! The worship leader part of me wanted to make sure my team member was comfortable, but the writer side of me couldn't pass this up. Think about it! How often have we stumbled over or missed things in our path just because we aren't paying attention or we're just busy being busy! Things like a friend who needs a hug, a prayer request once mentioned and now forgotten, or even the Lord's gentle nudging to come away with Him and rest. May I suggest that we pay more attention to what comes along our paths because it's quite possible the Lord put them there for a reason, even if it makes us stumble because maybe He needed to remind us of something. So, I know what I'm going to do first. The next time I'm at church I'm going straight to that storage room and I'm going to put up a great big sign that says, "Caution! Manger in path! When "stumbling" by please remember.......Christ was born for you!!"

I HAD LUNCH WITH MY CO-WORKERS THE OTHER DAY LIKE ALWAYS AND I SAT IN MY usual seat, which every one knows is the seat at the end of the table, next to the wall, facing the window. And they actually allow me to believe it really is MY seat! Everything was just fine until we stood up to leave and I realized the whole right side of my "behinder" was soaked! My first concern was.......WITH WHAT??? I did a quick subtle check. Not sticky...good! No odor...very good! Colorless...double good! Obviously water. Fortunately I was wearing black pants so it was not very noticeable, although my friends took advantage of the situation and I became the "butt" of some of their very funny jokes! Now, I realize this post so far has been a little "cheeky" (ha!) but on the serious side, let's think about this. How often do we make messes that someone else has to clean up? How often do we let something slip out of our hands (or out of our mouths) that was never meant to effect someone else, but it does. And how often do we let the problems in our lives "spill" over into the lives of others creating a mess for them? So when you find yourself in the middle of one of these situations and you're not sure you'll make it through, turn to the One Who rules over these messes and let Him clean up, wipe away, and make all things new! Because that's what He does! And don't be afraid to let your friends help out either. Mine have already started. There's hardly a lunch goes by that one of them doesn't say, "Jackie...CHECK YOUR CHAIR!!"

Jacqualine K. Boog

*M*YSELF AND TWO OF MY CO-WORKERS WENT DOWN TO THE CAFETERIA THE other morning to get water and juice. It's a daily ritual. On the way back we got on the elevator, chattering away, when I said, "Hey, are we moving?" One of the girls said, "Um…did anyone push the button?" And the rest of the conversation went something like this, "I didn't push the button! Did you push the button? Nope, I was never near the button! What button??" So we were basically standing there "spinning our wheels" so to speak and getting absolutely nowhere! (We did briefly consider pushing ALL the buttons and just riding the elevator for awhile and then thought better of that idea.) I can't tell you how often I feel like I'm spinning my wheels, feeling like for every 3 steps forward I take 10 back. Or like I work hard all day only to find my stack of things to do looking exactly the same or bigger! We've all been there. However, I can tell you what to do about it. For there is One who has promised to help carry these loads. In fact, He will carry you as well. And give you strength, endurance, and all that you need to accomplish your goals. How do I know this? Because He says so!! "Come to Me, all you who labor and are heavy laden, and I will give you rest." (Matthew 11:28) And now I will ask the question that everybody has been thinking….."Does her elevator go to the top floor??" Yes…yes it does! When I push the right button!!!

*T*HERE IS A HUGE METAL AWNING THAT COVERS THE ENTRANCE TO THE MEDICAL building where I work. And when the wind blows through it the most beautiful sound is created, almost like it's singing. Sometimes I'm tempted to stand under it and sing along, but that would just be weird! However, I will admit to humming along just to see if I can figure out what key it's in! (A personal challenge!) It makes me think about how we listen and what we hear. When I walk under the awning I hear the sound of music. Someone else might hear the sound of the wind. But more importantly, how do we listen to those who are speaking to us? When your family and friends speak, are you attentive to what they are saying? Do you hear what your pastor is speaking as he brings his message each week? Are you in tune with that still small voice that speaks so quietly to your heart from His? If so, then let them know. Speak words of love and affirmation to your family and friends. Give encouragement to your pastor as he seeks the Lord's word for you. (Trying to put a plug in here for you Pastor Mike!) And take time to be still so you can hear God's special sounds created just for you! And, maybe the next time the wind blows, I will stand under that awning and sing along. Or maybe not. It is, after all, a medical building and I could be "taken " to a floor where I don't work. One with a special room for those who randomly break into song for no apparent reason!!

*T*WO OF THE GUYS ON THE WORSHIP TEAM WERE TRYING TO FIGURE OUT THE chords to a song. And before I knew it, I was involved. I'd like to tell you we were working on a new contemporary Christian song, but, no, we were trying to figure out an old classic song, ♫Something♫ by the Beatles. There was one chord we just couldn't seem to figure out. The Beatles, although beautiful, used some most unusual transitions! It took awhile, but with some determination, perseverance (and a little help from the internet) we found the elusive chord. And, oh, what a feeling that is! Nothing can adequately describe it. It is utter satisfaction, a feeling of completeness, and your entire body just goes, "A-a-a-h-h-h!" ♫Imagine♫, if you will, the Lord seeking after the lost with that same determination and perseverance, searching for that elusive soul that needs to be in place for His song to be complete. And when the lost is found, I believe the angelic realm breathes a collective and satisfied, "A-a-a-h-h-h!" So stop hiding and let that ♫Long and Winding Road♫ become straight and narrow and enter into His song! Search no more for what you think is elusive and become complete in Him. He is, after all, the final chord in every song! You should have done it ♫Yesterday♫. You can still do it today! And for those of you who will now be singing these songs for the next couple of days……you're welcome!! Just ♫Let it Be♫!!

I RECENTLY WITNESSED A VERY UNUSUAL PHENOMENON FROM THE WINDOWS IN THE cafeteria where I work. Apparently, on a sunny day, the clouds will cast a shadow on the frozen lake making it appear like there is open water. And then the cloud moves and it looks like it closes in on itself and the "open water" disappears! I couldn't take my eyes off of it. As a matter of fact, I was sitting with my hands on the windowsill and my nose practically glued to the window. (Somewhat like a puppy with its nose pressed against the car window waiting to get out!) I was so enthralled with the whole thing that I was giving the girls a blow by blow narrative of the event. "Look! There's one! Oh, wait, now it's gone. There's another one moving to the right! This is amazing!" They finally convinced me we had to leave and nearly had to drag me away because I wanted to stay and watch this beautiful sight. Later, as I was thinking about this, I wondered why we don't have this same reaction to the greatness of God. Pastor Mike asked us Sunday morning, "How much do you want to know Jesus?" And I ask, enough to cling to the windowsills of Heaven in hopes of a glimpse of Him? Enough to stay in the same place for hours just to gaze at His beauty? Enough to shout to those around you, "Wow! Did you see that? He's amazing!" The cloud shadows are fascinating but nothing compares to the glory of God. He's just showing off with the beauty of the earth! Wait until the finale when all Heaven breaks loose!! That will be a show worth hanging around for!

*O*UR GRANDDAUGHTER LILY DOES EVERYTHING IN HER LITTLE LIFE WITH GUSTO. We nicknamed her Lily Bean but she is just way too cool for that. We now simply refer to her as "The Bean". She was at our house the other night and had her first piano lesson sitting in her Daddy's lap, watching his hands, and doing what he did. "The Bean" played with flare, with drama, with confidence, and with extreme gusto! She even added some beat boxing and at one point lifted her arms in the air as if to say, "Ta Da!" I'm convinced she's a genius because I'm pretty sure I heard the beginning of Beethoven's Fifth in the middle of her performance and who would have thought to put it there! Lily is happy, full of life, and content.....in whatsoever she does. Maybe we all need to take a lesson from "The Bean". I think as adults we too often allow the circumstances of life to rob us of the peace that God so freely gives in whatsoever the circumstance. So, how do we change this? Well, how 'bout we put a little more gusto in what we do? Or give ourselves a well deserved "Ta Da!" once in awhile? Personally, I may try to add in a line from Beethoven's Fifth when it's least expected! But, most importantly, let's all learn, like Lily, to sit in our Father's lap, let His hands guide ours, and learn to find peace and contentment in His everlasting love!

A FEW WEEKS AGO LARRY AND I WERE VICTIMS OF THE NOW INFAMOUS "BROKEN bridge". Our quaint little town has a draw bridge which is the quickest way in and out.....unless it's open! As the story goes, the powers that be were doing a test. The bridge got stuck open about 1/3 of the way up. Epic fail!! We arrived in the line up about 20 minutes after this happened and were told it would most likely be a 2-3 hour "fix". So we had the choice of waiting it out or driving 50 miles around the lake to our home which is literally about 6 blocks from where we were sitting in our car! So we did what most everybody else was doing and headed out of town to get back into town!! But the whole thing got me to thinking about our attitudes. Mine in particular which was getting progressively worse per mile traveled! I was upset at whoever decided it was a good idea to test the bridge on a Friday night at 9:00 P.M. I was frustrated with the time I felt we were wasting. And the more I fussed and fumed the more I realized I needed an attitude check. Epic fail!! Things don't always go exactly as planned, but we can "bridge the gap" of bad attitudes by taking Paul's advise to the Philippians and think on those things that are "pure" (a nice evening ride with my husband), "lovely" (our beautiful little town with it's cute little bridge), and "noble" (the guy trying to fix said bridge). So did my attitude change? Slightly. Until we pulled into town at 10:45 and found out the bridge had opened 5 minutes before that!! Grasping at straws here, but, maybe whatsoever is "just"?? Phil. 4:8 ☺

*T*HE OTHER DAY I KEPT FEELING LIKE SOMETHING WAS POKING MY BIG TOE, ALMOST like a small thumb tack. There didn't appear to be anything in my shoe and it would kind of come and go so I just ignored it. Well, at the end of the day I finally sat down, took my shoe off, took the insert out of my shoe (bad arches), and…..nothing! So I put everything back together and started to slip my foot in to my shoe and there it was! A small, pointy, sliver of wood sticking out of my sock! I had been focused on my shoe and never thought to check my sock! It made me think of the emotional hidden pain we all carry around and can't seem to find the source for it. Could it be we are looking in the wrong place? Are we choosing to ignore it thinking it will just go away? Are we just accepting it and hoping someday it won't be there any more? Maybe the best thing to do is to peel off the layers (including your socks if necessary) and try to find the true source of that pain. Do what you can to relieve it, but if you can't, turn it over to the One who can. The Lover of your soul, the Glory and the Lifter of your head. He will remove that thorn (or sliver) from your flesh (because He knows where it's at) and make all things new again! However, I'm pretty sure I'll probably have to sew the hole in my sock myself!

*T*HE BUILDING I WORK IN IS A MAZE OF STAIRWELLS, ELEVATORS, HALLWAYS AND I think a catacomb of tunnels in the basement! (The girls tell me it's a walking path, but I don't know!) It's because a long time ago someone decided to combine two buildings into one and the trail they left is not easy to follow…for some. If I am not with my "pack", I am lost. If they take a different route than usual I will inevitably turn the wrong way at some point and one of them will have to get me back in place. I rarely go anywhere alone except for food or a bathroom. (So if I had to survive on my own I could!) The girls have actually suggested I wear some kind of tracking system because they are constantly concerned that I will get lost somewhere and they will find me sitting in a corner crying, waiting for them to retrieve me! There was a time in my life that I was lost, but Somebody found me. I was blind and couldn't find my way and He put me back on the right path. I was curled up in a corner waiting for help and He reached out His hand and pulled me back into place. Who could do such a thing? An amazing God with amazing grace! So, will I eventually be able to find my way around the hospital? Probably not, especially since they keep moving things around. Will I be able to find my way to Heaven? You betcha!! Because that path is clearly marked!! ♥

*L*AST WEEKEND I MADE EASTER COOKIES. YOU KNOW THE KIND. THEY COME IN A box, frozen, already cut out and ready to bake in the oven. Then you decorate them with frosting from a can and sprinkles. (What? Isn't that how everybody makes fresh, home baked cookies?) Our grandkids Elliott and Brynn were here. Elliott was patiently waiting for a frosted cookie and Brynn was helping with the sprinkles. And she said, "Grandma! This bunny has been decapitated! His head is missing!" I said, "No, you're looking at him wrong. That's his butt!" You see, folks, it's all in the perspective and whether or not we have a positive outlook. Is the grass greener on the other side or does your brown grass need you to care for it? Is the glass half empty or did you just quench an intense thirst, and now there's more left for later! And here's the bottom line. The Lord promises to make it all good if we love Him. That's the deal. Love Him, life is good. Know Him, His mercies are yours every single day! Receive Him, life is yours forever! So, take care of the grass you walk on. Keep your glass full to the brim. And as far as the cookie goes….whether it was missing its head or its behind, it was still better than no cookie at all! And that's a positive outlook!

*I*HAVE A NECKLACE WITH A HEART ON IT THAT HAS, OVER TIME, DISCOLORED. AND I wonder how that happened. Did I mishandle it or not clean it enough? Or worse yet, did I try to clean it with the wrong kind of cleanser? I've been told if I gently wipe it with a special cloth it might restore it to its original color. But I'm also wondering about the heart that beats inside of me. Have I somehow let it get slightly discolored? Did I mishandle it by allowing life's hurts and disappointments to darken it? Have I not cleaned it enough by forgetting to ask for forgiveness, repent and let the love of God wash over it? Or worse yet, have I tried to clean it with the wrong cleanser using worldly things to try and hide the discoloration? God forgive me if I have! I'm speaking for myself here but I would rather let the Lord gently wipe away any stain with His gentle touch and rest in the assurance that He holds my heart inside of His own, radiant, beautiful and perfectly restored to its original color!!

*I*HAD TO CALL KINDLE SUPPORT THE OTHER DAY BECAUSE OF A PROBLEM I WAS having. I got a delightful young man who was eager to help. The first thing he said was, "Go to your home page and swipe down from the top. At the far right you'll see "more". Tap on that." I did as he requested and he checked out some settings on my device. He didn't see anything wrong and then asked me to go back to the home page, swipe down again, and this time tap "sync". Again, I did as instructed. He asked if it was doing anything. I said it was just twirling around. He said, "Tap more". So, I did. He asked again if it was doing anything and I said it was not. Just twirling. He said, "Tap more". And I said, "I am but how many times do you want…...oh wait….. did you mean tap ON "more"? Because I've been tapping repeatedly (tap more) on sync!" At this point, he began to laugh. I mean like he couldn't speak laugh! The next thing I said was, "Do NOT tell your buddies about this!! I'll sound like the lady who thought her CD holder was for her cup!!" Which was followed by another round of uncontrollable laughter. I also mentioned the color of my hair and now I'm pretty sure the guy is rolling on the floor unable to breathe. You're probably wondering why I confess to these little stories. It's because laughter truly is one of the best medicines. Don't believe me? Go ahead and laugh…. and then laugh "MORE"!!!! ☺

WE WENT UP TO SEE OUR SON MATTHEW AND HIS WIFE JENNIFER LAST WEEKEND. Oh…who am I kidding! We went to see our granddaughter Lily Bean! Lily has a new found passion for a few of her stuffed animals. And when you hand one to her, she gives it a hug and says, "A-w-w-w!" (or the equivalent there of with a pacifier in one's mouth!) and she shows each animal love straight from her little heart. So, I was sitting on the floor with her and handing her an animal one at a time. And she gave each one a hug and an "A-w-w-w!" and the next thing I know, I'm engulfed in a group hug with a piggy, a bunny, a small elephant in pajamas and….Lily! I cannot describe how loved I felt as she wrapped her arms around all of us and said, "A-w-w-w!" (And I might add, out of the whole bunch in this hug, I'm pretty sure I was her favorite!) Do you have any idea how comforting the arms of the Lord are? Do you know that when He wraps His children in His arms, out of the whole bunch, you are His favorite! And you….and you…. and you! And do you understand how much He cares when He whispers "A-w-w-w!" and shows you love straight from His great, big heart? Because in that moment you will not be able to describe how loved you feel! I suggest we all take our cue from Lily Bean and remember to give hugs, comforting words, and love straight from our hearts…minus the pacifier. Most of us couldn't pull that off!!

I WAS WRITING OUT MY "TO DO" LIST FOR TODAY AND IT LOOKED SOMETHING LIKE this: Laundry, pay bills, fix Jesus loves me, send worship list to team. Wait! What? Fix Jesus loves me? I don't think so! What could possibly need fixing about that?? The truth of the matter is, I needed to fix the ending to a new Chris Tomlin song I'm working on called "Jesus Loves Me". (I make lists that only I would understand.) When I looked at it later, it kind of made me laugh, and then it made me realize again something wonderful......how perfect His love is! It is pure, endless and without measure! It is mine forever and always! And most of all, there is nothing I could do to change the love He has for me! I'm sure He looks at me once in a while and goes, "Excuse me! What were you thinking there??" Or, "Hello! Did I NOT say I would take care of that?" But He still loves me, all the time, every time, in spite of my shortcomings. So, I'll fix the ending to my song, but I'm not changing anything about His love for me - except receive and embrace it! Forever and always! So when you get your next "to do" list ready, remember to include "Jesus loves me" right at the top just to remind yourself that He always has and He always will! And there is absolutely nothing to fix about that!

*L*ARRY BOUGHT ME A BEAUTIFUL NECKLACE WHILE WE WERE UP NORTH. ACTUALLY, the truth is, I said, "I want that." And he said, "Okay." I mean we were, after all, in Jackie's World and I pretty much reign as queen when we're there. Anyway, it's a very delicate cut out of the Mighty Mac encircled by "hammered" silver. And every time I look at it I smile because it reminds me of a place that is very special to me. A place where the fragrance and beauty of the lakes soothe me. A place where the majesty of the Mackinaw Bridge amazes me. A place where I can breathe a little easier and live for awhile at a slower pace. But as much as I love Mackinaw, I know of another place that is even more special. A secret place. A hiding place. It's beauty and majesty will astound you. The fragrance there is like no other. And I truly am a princess in this place…a daughter of the most high King. I don't have to drive miles to get there. I only need to whisper His name - Jesus - and I am instantly in a place where my breathing becomes easier, and my pace begins to match His. And the funny thing is, I don't need a necklace to look at to remind me of this. On the contrary, I only need His gaze to fix on me!

*O*N OUR RECENT TRIP UP NORTH I TOOK SOME PICTURES FROM BENEATH THE Mackinaw Bridge which for some reason fascinated me. (Oh great.... does that make me a troll??) It's not particularly beautiful but it is the foundation for the entire bridge. If there wasn't a "beneath the bridge" there would be no support for the bridge above and no way it could carry all it needs to hold every single day. And every time I thought about "beneath the bridge" I couldn't help but think about the phrase "beneath the cross" where we go to stand on our foundation knowing it will provide all the support for everything we need to carry every single day! Knowing that its sturdiness will never let us down. Knowing that every crossing we make will be under girded by its strength. And just as standing at the foot of the bridge gave me a different perspective as I looked up and saw the wonders of the Mighty Mac, so standing at the foot of the cross gives me a new perspective as I look up and see the wonders of a Mighty God. Two bridges.....one connecting the lower part of the state to the upper..... the other connecting man to God. And that is a picture worth a thousand words!

I'M GOING TO SHARE A TRUE STORY WITH YOU AND I'LL BE HONEST, I'M NOT VERY proud of it. Most of you know I'm a big fan of Bath and Body Works and have an arsenal of their products to choose from in my daily bathing routines. A few months back I bought a moisturizing cream, because it was on sale, smelled great, and promised to "moisturize my skin with luxurious silk proteins and cashmere extract, taking me-time to the next level"! Who wouldn't want that, right? Anyway, this stuff was so creamy and silky I had a hard time getting it to smooth into my skin, almost like a layer of it remained on top and kind of left me with a little bit of a sticky feeling. However, I smelled amazing and I was confident it was doing it's job as I could still feel it working the next day. Just out of curiosity, I decided to do a little research on this product (because, you know, moisturizers can be used improperly) and much to my dismay, I found a line I had missed before. (And here comes the not very proud part!) "Skin feels deeply hydrated and ultra-pampered even after you RINSE!!" What?? I have been moisturizing my skin with very creamy SOAP!!! As I shared my revelation with my husband he just laughed, rolled his eyes with that "I'm so glad you're my wife" expression, and then said, "I guess we should all be thankful that you didn't get caught in the rain without a jacket and begin to "bubble up" on your exposed skin!" Is there a moral to this story? Nope! Does it give me a good laugh? Every time I think about it! Does it have a spiritual application? Um…...cleanliness is next to Godliness?? ☺

*T*HERE'S A YOUNG MAN WHO ATTENDS OUR CHURCH WITH HIS FAMILY WHEN HE'S not at college. He is truly a "gentle giant" as he is about 6'9" tall and his heart is as large as his stature is tall. Like his father, he is a drummer, and when he's home, he plays drums in his father's place for our worship team (probably just a bit better but I won't go there!) and this last Sunday he happened to be home. During the offertory I usually play a little "traveling music" and Pastor Mike will normally encourage people to stand and greet someone. But this Sunday he told them to give someone a hug. As I'm standing there playing and watching friends greet and hug each other, I see my young friend (he's kind of hard to miss) coming towards the platform. And then he did something that melted my heart! He came up and stood beside me and said, "Jackie, I'm gonna hug you!" And then he brought his 6'9" frame down to my 5'3" size (seriously, you can barely see me above my music stand) and he wrapped his arms around me in a gentle hug. I couldn't speak. I just stood there, still playing, grinning from ear to ear! I felt so special! I felt so loved! Thank you Zach for reminding me that whether you are short or tall, young or old, there is rarely an occasion where a hug is not a good thing! It eases your burdens. It lifts your spirits. It just plain makes you feel good. So now, I will remind all of you that a hug is a very good thing!! Give them out freely and often! Unless you're a bear! If you're a bear you should only hug another bear! Don't hug me!!!

WE MET OUR SON MATTHEW, HIS WIFE JEN, AND OUR GRANDDAUGHTER LILY for dinner the other night and asked if we could take Lily shopping with us giving them a little time to themselves. Matthew had to think about it and kind of reluctantly agreed. We got Lily all buckled in her car seat and thought we were good to go, when Lily gave her dad that, "Wait a minute! You're not coming with us?" look and all of a sudden in Matthew's eyes we became totally incapable of taking care of our own grandchild! And then the instructions began! "Make sure her seat is buckled in right! Tighten it up a little! Sanitize the shopping cart! And for Heaven's sake, don't let her fall out of the cart!" (Okay, in his defense that was a legitimate concern. He did fall out of a shopping cart once while on my watch! But I'm almost certain his brother Mark pushed him!) We had a wonderful time and Lily survived her first shopping excursion with Grandma and Grandpa. But I kept thinking about Matthew's concerns over who was watching his child. Do you realize your Father in Heaven has the same concerns? So He sent the Good Shepherd to tend His flock and you can be sure He will take exceptional care of you. He will keep you wrapped (buckled) in His love. He will keep you washed (clean) by His blood! And if you're prone to riding in shopping carts, He will be riding right behind you, grinning and saying, "Yep….this one belongs to Me!!"

I HAVE BEEN EXPERIENCING AN INTERESTING PHENOMENON ALMOST EVERY MORNING. When I open my Bible for my daily devotional, I smell baby vitamins. (And those from my generation will remember that distinct smell!) I know it sounds weird but it's true! It only lasts a moment and then it's gone. It honestly seems to be coming from my Bible but I become like a bloodhound on my bed anyway sniffing everything trying to see if I can find another source. But I have been unable to do so! So, I've decided to not try and understand it but instead embrace it as a gift from God. Because it brings back sweet memories of my grown up sons who were once little babies needing those vitamins. And it also reminds me of the fact that I need the daily "nutrients" from God's word. That just as my body would suffer without a daily dose of proper vitamins, so my spirit would suffer without a daily dose of God. So, from now on when I get a whiff of that fragrance, I will breathe deeply and let His daily bread sink into my mind and spirit and feel secure knowing He is the only source for the very sustenance I need. And if I could put that in a pill form and sell it in a bottle...I would call it "One-a-Dei"! Ya, go ahead and roll your eyes but you know that's cute!!

*M*Y WATCH RECENTLY STOPPED WORKING SO WE GOT A NEW BATTERY FOR IT BUT that didn't help at all. It's apparently broke. But, not to worry. I have plenty of other watches. Except everyone I pulled out to wear was not working either! And then I realized the clock in my bedroom hadn't been working for days. And we had a power surge that made my clock radio on the bed stand stop working. So basically all the clocks around me stopped! I discussed this with my son Matthew who asked, "Wow mom! Have you recently had an MRI or something?? Any paper clips or other stuff sticking to you??" (He's such a funny kid!) But I am a clock watcher and often think about the time. So, I'm asking myself, "Does anybody really know what time it is? Does anybody really care?" (Sorry…generation slip!) And then I wondered "If I could save time in a bottle". (Oops…same generation!) But then I got serious and was thinking about Godly time. Where a day is as a thousand to Him. Where time is no longer measured in seconds and in minutes but in Hallelujahs and Holy Holy's. And where time has absolutely no meaning as we are able to sit at the feet of a timeless Lord! Eternal time. That's what we need to be thinking about, preparing for, yearning for. Everlasting to everlasting! But in the mean "time", just wondering, "Are you going to Scarborough Fair? Parsley, sage, rosemary, and thyme!" (I'm sorry! I couldn't help myself. I just couldn't!!) ☺

*I*RECENTLY DISCOVERED THAT SOMETHING HAS BEEN MUNCHING ON MY PRETTY, purple, potted pansies that were hanging in a basket in my front yard. Not only that, but he trotted around to the back and left a nice little pile of purple, poo pellets! (Just kidding….they weren't nice!) And I say "he" because no lady would leave a mess like that in public for all to see!! So I put 2 and 2 together and came up with 1 deer. And those of you who know me will understand how lucky he was to find my flowers were still alive and edible! I was a little miffed with this creature but then realized he really didn't mean any harm and was actually out of his home territory since I live in town! He just wanted something sweet to eat. Which made me think of how often I get a little miffed with people. Why would they do that? Did they have to speak to me that way? What were they thinking? When maybe the truth is, they really didn't mean to do any harm and might have been a little out of their own territory. Perhaps what was said or done was taken completely the wrong way and they honestly thought they were being "sweet". We probably all have "dear" friends that are often misunderstood. So let's learn to give grace to the deer who munch on our flowers and to the friends who just sometimes say the wrong thing at the wrong time. A word of caution however. There are those who tend to leave a "pile" of stuff behind them. Avoid stepping in that! You will only create a whole other set of problems! Just sayin……

*M*Y CHILDHOOD WAS NOT THE BEST. IT WASN'T THE WORST, BUT IT WASN'T THE best. And sometimes I have a hard time finding a good memory which for some reason seems important to me right now. As the eldest child I kind of feel like the keeper of the family memories. I went for a walk the other night and saw a young family playing outside. One little girl was already in her pajamas giggling and running through the yard while her daddy chased her. As I watched this, I instantly smelled popcorn. Not in the air, but in my head. And a memory flashed through my mind so quickly I almost lost it. I was a little girl again and Mom was getting my brother, sister, and I into our pajamas and Dad was making popcorn. But we didn't go to bed and the popcorn didn't go in a bowl. It went into a big grocery bag and came along with us in the old station wagon to the drive-in movie. We played on the swings until the movie started, and we ate popcorn out of the bag (which was better than any we could have bought) while watching the movie, and eventually we snuggled up and fell asleep in the back of the car (hence the pajamas ahead of time) while Mom and Dad watched part of the second movie. Such a sweet, comforting memory! Thank you family on my walk for allowing me to be that little girl again if only for a few fleeting moments. And now go out and make your own memories. You'll want to keep them for another day when they will make you smile and think about little kids in pajamas, popcorn in a grocery bag, and movies watched from the back of a station wagon. Hold tight to them! You might be the keeper of your family memories some day!

*I*WAS TRYING TO REACH AN INSURANCE COMPANY AT WORK. I WANTED TO SPEAK TO a person but couldn't get past the birth date input. They said it was invalid. I knew it was correct. I kept trying to follow their directions and was getting nowhere. I even resorted to hitting the zero repeatedly which only served to anger them because their reply was, "We're sorry. We cannot help you. Good-bye!" All I wanted to do was finish one more thing! After about 30 minutes of this I came to the conclusion that they had a problem, not me, and decided to wait and try again in the morning when I was less frustrated. So, the next day I began the process again. I went through all the prompts and when it came to entering the birth date I actually listened and heard, "Enter the birth date in a 6 digit format." Oops! I had been using an 8 digit format!! In my haste the night before I had failed to listen and follow their directions creating my own problem! And now I'm wondering have I done this with other things? Like God's word for instance. In my haste to finish one more thing am I failing to listen and follow His directions? Like, "Come to Me all you who labor and are heavy laden and I will give you rest." Did I miss "come"? Or, "But seek first the kingdom of God and His righteousness and all these things shall be added to you." Did I skip "Seek first"? And, lastly, "If My people who are called by My name will humble themselves and pray and seek My face, and turn from their wicked ways, then I will hear from Heaven and will forgive their sin and heal their land." Did I pass over humbleness and repentance? So don't just rush quickly through what could be important. Slow down, listen, and follow directions. Especially His!! I guarantee you will save yourself a lot of frustration!!

WELL, MY DEAR FRIEND, MS. DEER, THAT I WROTE ABOUT A FEW WEEKS AGO IS back. If you recall I was pretty sure it was a male but it has come to my attention that there are two fawns in our area, hence, I now believe she is female with an unusual appetite for my flowers. She has previously only nibbled on the petals but this time she ate the entire plant! She chewed on those things until there was nothing left but the little stubs sticking up out of the dirt! Or maybe she's not eating them. Since she's a girl, maybe she took the flowers and fashioned herself a nice little garland and is now parading around the neighborhood wearing it like a crown! I have some dear friends who, like my plant, are feeling kind of chewed up right now. The wind has been knocked right out of their sails. And even though I no longer work with them I still share their pain as it was only a few months ago I was there and would be in that same boat without a sail. And, ladies I know you're hurting and worried and concerned. But here's a thought. How about if we think about these things as flowers. Lovely buds of hope that will open into flowers like ashes into beauty. And take a cue from my deer friend and fashion them into a precious little garland and imagine wearing them as a crown. A crown of God's goodness and grace. For He is faithful and true. And He will use all things for good. It's His promise. You can believe it! And I would also like to remind you of a lesson we learned together a few years ago. If you can sing a rousing version of "You put the lime in the coconut and shake it all up"…it will make you smile. And if you can get your co-workers to join you in a conga line while you sing it, well, that's just plain laugh out loud funny!! Keep smiling ladies! Keep laughing! Keep dancing! Keep believing!!

I LOVE WHEN ALL MY KIDS ARE HOME FOR A MEAL. I LOVE TO FEED THEM! I LOVE watching them eat their favorite foods so much so that sometimes I barely eat myself! It just makes my heart grow bigger and bigger watching them become so satisfied. And I love to hear their laughter and how they tease each other over who is mom's favorite. (You know who you are wink, wink!) In that moment nothing else matters. My kids are home, they're happy and they're fed!! Now imagine, if you will, as the Lord prepares His banquet table. He prepares it with all of our favorites because He knows exactly what they are. He makes sure there is plenty to go around. Then He waits and watches as His children begin to gather around and feast at His table. And in that moment He has eyes for nothing else. He loves the sound of our laughter and He loves when we're all together. None of us have to wonder who His favorite is because that list includes all of us and is written on His heart. He claps His hands, He rejoices over us, and, if possible, His heart grows bigger and bigger! Because He loves when His children are home, they're happy, and they're well fed. So don't hesitate. Come to the table of the Lord and feast on that which is good. Always and forever good; prepared just for you!

*A*FEW SUNDAYS AGO I WAS TALKING TO PASTOR MIKE AND ONE OF THE GUYS ON the worship team. As I was talking I was trying to get my headset/ microphone on which goes behind my neck, over my ears, and then the battery pack goes on my waist. For some reason I couldn't get the cord to wrap around from the back to the front and I was trying to rearrange it to get it untangled. I finally stopped and said, "What is wrong with this thing?" Pastor Mike said, "I don't think anything is wrong with it but this has become very entertaining!" Which I'm sure was true as I had now slipped into the "I ran into a spider web and I can't get out" routine flailing about at nothing! But, the thing is, I was trying to fix something that didn't need fixing. The cord was fine where it was. I wonder how often and how silly we sometimes look trying to untangle ourselves from imaginary problems, especially to God. I mean, it seems like we spend a lot of time trying to straighten out, unravel, or push around situations in our lives when honestly there's nothing wrong with where they are! And I can imagine the Lord saying, "Hey...will you quit struggling and let me get you untangled?" So here's the lesson learned: Sometimes things are okay right where they are. (Stop flailing about at nothing!) The more you fuss the more tangled up you'll get. (Stop fussing and leave the untangling to God.) And ALWAYS try to be a source of entertainment to those around you, because when you smile...well....you know...the whole world smiles with you!! (Some of you just sang that last line like you were in a Broadway musical...didn't ya!)

Jacqualine K. Boog

*L*AST SUNDAY WE WERE DOING A NEW SONG THAT HAS A NICE, BIG POWERFUL section in the middle and then quiets down and ends on a nice soft chorus. We had just finished the big powerful middle section and were bringing it down for the soft ending when I realized my drummer was "powering up" again with a big lead in, apparently heading in a different direction. And everybody knows when your drummer comes back with a powerful rhythm lead in, you better have a powerful sound to follow that up with. Now, folks, I had about 2 seconds (or 2 beats) to decide what to do. And in those split seconds I did the only thing a good leader could do, I followed the drummer! Because, it's a well known fact that where the drummer goes, you follow. If you don't the only one to come out of this situation looking good is, you guessed it, the drummer! (Every drummer I know just shouted, "Hallelujah! Preach it sister!") So I went back to repeat the "power" section and everybody followed. (Fortunately, I didn't have to think about what chord was next because we were in the key of "C". I could play any of the white keys and pretty much be right!) Nailed it! We were ready in season and out. And isn't that what the Lord calls us to do? Be ready in season and out? If He changes direction, we better be ready to follow. If He opens a new door, we better go through! And if He creates a new path, start walking on it! Don't hesitate, don't think about it, just follow the "power" source! He is, after all, the ultimate leader! So, as the good word says, take up your cross (or drumsticks as the case may be) and follow Him! He may surprise you once in awhile but He will never lead you wrong!!

*M*Y EVENING WALKS HAVE BEEN INSPIRATIONAL LATELY AS THE LORD GIVES ME wonderful word pictures. And so I set out the other night with my mind open waiting for what little thing the Lord might show me. I got about ½ block from my house and stopped dead in my tracks! For there, hanging just inches from my body, was a not so little, black, ugly spider. (And by "not so little" I mean HUGE…because ALL spiders are HUGE!) I hesitated for mere seconds as to which path to choose. Since I wasn't sure where its web was, I didn't want to go around it and continue my walk only to find it had somehow attached itself to me and was now dangling from behind me like a tail on a kite! I obviously wasn't going to try and remove it from my path! And so I let out an audible "E-W-W!" just to let the spider know how disgusted I was with him, took one giant step back and ran to the other side of the street! (Probably won't walk on my side of the street again until next year just to be sure!) And what did the Lord show me from this? That we all have "problems" that get dangled in front of us every day and we have to choose how to deal with them. We can try to remove them from our path. We can stand there paralyzed and hope it will go away. Or we can do as I did, run away quickly! But there's a better option. We can go to the One who knows our beginning from our end and ask Him to show us which way to go. We can ask Him for grace, wisdom and understanding and He will set us on the proper path to overcome any problem. And, just a suggestion, I wouldn't try the "run around it" option because if you get caught in its ugly web and end up with your problems following behind you like a tail on a kite….well…that's just not a pretty sight!

A FEW OF US FROM THE WORSHIP TEAM WERE WORKING ON AN IN EAR MONITOR system. Which basically means no amps, no monitors, everything is heard through your personal headset. Which really cleans up the sound! No excess noise from the platform. (Sound techniques 101....lesson 3. You're welcome!) We only had one headset to use so one guy was listening to see if the instruments were coming through. I was playing the keyboard with absolutely no sound coming from it which, I might add, I was doing very well until....I made a mistake! How did I know since there was no sound? I could feel it. I just instinctively knew and I looked down and sure enough...my fingers were on the wrong notes. So I did what every good musician does. I owned it! I said, "Oops! My bad!" but no one really knew without the sound except one, the guy with the headset. How often do we make secret mistakes that we think no one else notices? A bad word slips between our lips, a bit of gossip whispered to just one other, an attitude that you think is hidden but some clearly see it. And you think probably no one really noticed it...except One, He who has the big "headset" in Heaven, whose "ears" are always tuned to everything we do. The One who listens, Who knows, and Who loves just the same. And unlike my sound guy who said nothing, the Lord will gently let you know when you've made a mistake. He will hear your admission of, "Oops! My bad!" and say, "You've owned it, now change it!" And when He does you will instinctively know what to do and soon you'll be making that sweet sound again! And probably won't mind if more than one is listening! ♫♫♫

I GOT A NEW ELECTRIC DENTAL AIR FLOSSER. THIS THING IS AMAZING! IT SHOOTS small bursts of air and mouthwash between your teeth. Now, there are two important things to remember when using this product. 1. Your aim has got to be true. 2. And this can't be stressed enough......CLOSE YOUR MOUTH WHEN USING! Before putting any mouthwash in it, I looked it over thoroughly, made sure I knew where the on/off button was, and figured out the exact placement for optimum "shooting". I then locked and loaded, took one more look at it, and proceeded to......spray myself in the face! I accidentally hit the "trigger"! That kind of shocked me and while I was trying to get my bearings, I shot it again this time spraying the bathroom mirror! I started laughing at myself and how ridiculous this was and managed to shoot twice more straight into the air! At this point everything in the bathroom was clean and minty fresh except my teeth! I finally managed to get it in my mouth, targeted the area and fired....completely forgetting rule #2! After cleaning off the bathroom mirror a second time, I started the process again. However, I now noticed a fascinating side effect. With my mouth closed, the little bursts of air really had nowhere to go and were blowing up my cheeks like a tuba player trying to hit the big notes in John Philip Sousa's "Stars and Stripes Forever"!! I have no further comment on that! When I finally came out of the bathroom looking a little flushed and somewhat damp, my husband asked, "What have you been doing in there?" I replied, "Flossing my teeth! Why??" ☺

WE MET MATTHEW, JEN, AND, OF COURSE, LILY BEAN FOR DINNER AT WENDY'S last night. I was so excited to see Lily that I only let them get halfway through the door. Lily's at that stage where she gets a little shy. She knows who I am but when she hasn't seen me in awhile she will back away from me. So I got down close to her level and tried to coax her into my arms. She looked at me, backed up and turned to go the other way, and….. ran right smack into the door. (Which is another direct confirmation that she does, in fact, take after her Grandma! I've ran into my share of doors!) Now, look out for some preaching 'cause I'm about to turn this into a salvation message! (Matthew calls it "Jesus-izing" his daughter. I call it seeing through the innocence of a child!) But here's what I believe. The Lord is always calling out to His children. He gets down on their level and tries to coax them into His arms. And I think His children see Him as someone they know but they're unsure, not certain, and a little shy because they haven't spent a lot of time with him. But, the truth is….He is your Father. He knows you to the point that every hair on your head is numbered. (For some that's a low count, but they are numbered just the same!) He desires to spend time with you and wants you to know Him well enough that you are comfortable with and eager to be in His presence. I can tell you without a doubt my friends that this is the time to run into those arms, accept the love of Jesus and for Heaven's sake…stop running into doors!!! There! Done preaching!! I feel better, don't you?? ☺

WHILE MY HUSBAND LARRY AND I WERE UP NORTH WE OBSERVED A FLOCK OF geese. Or is it a gaggle of geese? Doesn't matter.....that's not the point. We would see them in different places in the same area and there was always something a little out of place in the group. There was a single seagull hanging out with the entire bunch of geese everywhere they went. He was a goose "wanna-be"! If the geese swam in the water, he went swimming with them. If they waddled on to the sand, he waddled up there as well. And if they searched around for food, he did the same. (Although I don't think he was as picky about what he was eating as they were!) It didn't appear that the geese minded and I'm pretty sure the seagull didn't even notice. And that's the way it should be! God created us all unique and different and yet able to "flock" together. In fact, doesn't He encourage us to love one another, to fellowship as a group, and to look at the heart not the appearance? (And that little seagull had a heart of gold to put up with all that honking!) So, if you're not sure where you fit in, don't be a "wanna-be". Find yourself a "gaggle" of believers! Jump right in and join the flock! They will welcome you. They will find the best parts in you. And they will definitely feed you! Wasn't it a group of believers who organized the first pot luck? A fish fry I believe!! ☺

Jacqualine K. Boog

I WAS DOWN AT THE PARK A FEW WEEKS AGO AND THERE WAS A LITTLE BOY, MAYBE 3-4 years old, running around the band shell and up and down the grassy hills. His grandpa was trying to keep up with him and repeatedly said, "I am NOT going to chase you!" Which only prompted the little guy to start running again, stop and wait for his grandpa to get within a few feet of him and then take off at the pace of speed racer. Grandpa, on the other hand was "chasing" him at about the speed of the tortoise from the famous race with the hare! But every time he got close to the little guy, and by close I mean there was no way he was going to grab him, the scenario would repeat itself as the little boy ran out of his grandpa's reach and grandpa stood there long enough to proclaim his declaration one more time of "not chasing him" and then, in fact, chase him at his slow but sure pace. So let me ask you this. What is your pace or speed in your chase after the Lord? You cannot have an "I'm NOT going to chase You!" attitude. Because unlike this little boy, God absolutely wants to be caught. As a matter of fact, He will wait as long as it takes for you to catch Him and even runs towards you before you can get close to Him! And you can't be chasing after Him at a tortoise pace either. Your pursuit of Him must be relentless! Absolutely no dragging of the feet. I promise when you find that place of being caught up in His arms, you will no longer want to run because the chase will become as simple as calling His name! Go ahead and try it. It's a race worth running when the prize is Him!

I'VE BEEN THINKING ABOUT A CHILD'S LAUGHTER AND WHAT A DELIGHTFUL SOUND that is. Which then made me think about how we'll do almost anything (including silly faces, goofy sounds, and clown-like antics) to keep that laughter going just because it makes your heart so full. But, I also thought about a child's tears and how we suddenly become very serious in their need for comfort. When a little one is crying and you're holding them close to you for comfort, there is no more gratifying feeling then when those tears become fewer, their breathing becomes calmer, and they rest easy because they know they are in the arms of someone who loves them deeply. So what does this have to do with anything? Not a lot. Except it made me think about God's unconditional love for us. How He delights in us and how His heart fills with joy when He hears the sound of His child laughing. And yet, when we cry He gets very serious and immediately envelopes us in those arms of love until our tears become fewer, our breathing becomes calmer, and we are resting easy in the arms of One who loves us deeply. Mmm…I guess I was wrong. It does have to do with something. It has to do with a Heavenly Father who laughs with you in your joy, captures your tears in your sorrow, and will do anything to let you know He's got you!! "He will rejoice over you with gladness, He will quiet you with His love, He will rejoice over you with singing." Zephaniah 3:17

I GOT MYSELF INTO A SLIGHT PREDICAMENT THE OTHER NIGHT. I WAS TRYING TO PUT my coat on but instead of one arm at a time (like I usually do) I decided to put both arms straight up and let it slide down and into place. Why? I'm not sure but it didn't work! I think it was because I was wearing a sweatshirt which was not conducive to "sliding". So I ended up stuck in my coat! My arms were halfway through the arm holes and somehow the very large hood and part of the back came over my head and hung down the front capturing me inside and I couldn't find my way out. I tried wriggling around a bit to no avail. I tried lifting my shoulders to hoist the coat up and over but it only got caught on my face! And the only help my husband gave me was to say, "Hold on just a minute. I can't find my camera!!" I'm not going to lie to you folks…it wasn't a pretty sight! The only comparison that comes to mind is that of a blow up character for your yard that has lost part of its air; arms dangling, head down! I finally quite struggling and sort of relaxed a little and the whole thing slid right into place! So I wondered how I could apply this to every day life or what spiritual wisdom I could gain and decided it would be with the following questions. Have you ever been stuck in a predicament you can't find your way out of? Be still and wait on the One who will always guide you through. Have you ever felt like the wind has been let out of your sails? Let the breath of the Holy Spirit fill you up again. Have you ever felt foolish because of the choices you've made? Then for Heaven's sake…just put your coat on one arm at a time!

WE GOT TO TAKE CARE OF "THE BEAN" LAST NIGHT WHILE MAMMA AND DADDY were at a Christmas party. Matthew had recently commented that Lily is a little "active". But what 18 month old isn't? Right? I raised boys! I can handle this! So we came in prepared with one of Lily's favorite meals from Subway. I made the mistake of giving her a couple of chips with her sandwich and now that's all she wanted. I wasn't going to give her anymore but she used sign language to ask for them! She signed the word "more" and then the word "please"! And now I'm like, "How cute is that!" and I just kept giving her chips!! So basically she had applesauce and chips for dinner. I got her cleaned up and out of her high chair and she took off at warp speed. I was trying desperately to keep up with her but I was losing the battle quickly. Her first stop was the Christmas tree where she somehow managed to squirm so far back and under I couldn't get her out. I bribed her with my cell phone! (She loves taking selfies!!) Now the next adventure is a bit of a blur but somehow she opened the kitchen gate and was heading through the kitchen and up the stairs. I managed to grab her and get her on the other side of the gate. As I was latching it up again I couldn't find her and looked down just in time to see her wriggling through the cat door in the gate! And then she was off again with me trailing behind her! (I did NOT go through the cat door!) I finally had her in my arms and on the right side of the gate. And here is the topper, literally! She got hold of the cat's dish which had two parts, a stand and the dish. She kept picking the whole thing up and I kept grabbing it back and telling her no. On the third attempt I only got hold of the stand. I turned around to find Lily wearing the bowl like a hat! There she was standing there in her nightgown, a metal bowl on her head and little ringlets hanging from beneath it just looking at me like, "What?" I lost it right then and there. I just lifted up my hands, shook my head, scooped her into my arms and admitted she had bested me. Lily Bean one! Grandma zero!!

I HAVE A SOFT, WARM, BLANKET THAT I ADD ON TOP OF MY NORMAL BLANKETS EVERY night. And when I make the bed in the morning, the last thing I do is fold this blanket and lay it at the foot of the bed. Then I lean over the bed with my hand sinking into the blanket and smooth over the covers. Every time I do this I leave a perfect handprint in my blanket which is kind of like an image of myself, a sign that I've been there. It will remain there unless I choose to brush it away. Every day when I pray I ask the Lord to go before me and to keep His hand upon me and I envision His hand on my back just like I can see my hand print on my blanket. And His image will remain with me unless I choose to brush it away. A true sign that He has gone before me and that He has already been there. His handprint was on the stable that housed the Baby King as He slept and it was on the stone that was rolled from the tomb when death became life forever more! And His handprint is on us. Through the good and the bad. When we doubt every decision we make and when we rejoice in every victory that becomes ours. Forever and always, from His throne to our hearts (a spiritual version of to the moon and back)! And here's the thing. The Lord's handprint is not just a partial image, it's the whole package. All He is for all you need. You have the choice.....you can let it remain or you can brush it away. Choose wisely, my friends, especially this time of year as we once again have the opportunity to accept the love of a Baby King born in a manger held in the Hand of God.

*E*VERYONE KNOWS THAT INSIDE EVERY MAN, YOUNG OR OLD, IS A LITTLE BOY STILL wanting to play games. I was witness to this very fact yesterday at my son Matthew's house. It started with a discovery that the wind storm the day before had left a plastic snowman stranded in the top of a tree in Matthew's backyard. I saw it as a photo op. Matthew saw it as a challenge. I went out toward the tree with my cell phone. Matthew went with an extremely long stick, a look of determination and a hint of a smile playing on his lips. His first attempt to free the snowman was piñata style. He jumped and jumped while swinging and whacking at the thing with every leap. His only accomplishment was to break off the end of his stick. Next he tried what looked like Don Quixote chasing windmills. Matthew started a ways back from the tree, began running, and then did sort of a skip, hop, leap routine in an attempt to skewer the snowman. Notta! That piece of plastic just waved at him and grinned from what was left of his smile! He finally managed to get half of it down which he brought to me on his stick and told me to stand on it so he could pull it off. At this point I was laughing so hard I couldn't see Matthew, let alone the stick. I placed my foot firmly on the edge of the snowman and Matthew pulled but nothing released. Until he said, "Mom, you're standing on the stick!!" Oops! My bad! Approaching the tree one last time, Matthew tried a more gentle approach, sort of slipping the stick through the loop it had made and lifted. Finally success! Sort of….the silly thing came off and landed on the limb beneath it. Matthew had to repeat this procedure 3 times and 3 times Frosty floated down to a limb beneath it finally blowing over to a shorter tree where he was easily retrieved. Matthew went in the house satisfied with his quest. I went in trying to remove the mascara now trailing down my cheeks! Thank you Matthew for one of the best Christmas gifts ever... the gift of laughter!!

*I*WAS AT WAL-MART LAST WEEK ON ONE OF THEIR BUSIEST NIGHTS. I FOUND A checkout line that appeared to be moving at a fairly good pace. There were only two customers ahead of me and all seemed good until the cashier shouted, "Manager!". Oh, oh! Not a good sign! He called the manager twice more before he actually got to me. I was surprisingly calm under the circumstances. The lady in front of me was not. She was silently struggling and I could see it on her face. She mumbled something about someone waiting for her and already being upset and then said, "This should not be happening! I need to get out of here!" And I recognized the look on her face. I knew what she was feeling. The cashier ended up needing to re-ring her items which he did while apologizing over and over about the wait. That was the proverbial last straw! She never looked directly at me but I said very slowly and very calmly, "Breathe in, breath out". She closed her eyes and breathed a little slower. The guy behind the counter continued to talk a mile a minute with his apologies and I said to him, "It would probably be best if you would stop talking to her right now". And then I told her she was going to be outside in the fresh air in just a few minutes. When her purchase was finally done, she turned to leave, looked at me and simply said, "Thank you." I smiled at her. I understood. Because I have been there. And in that moment I was reminded of God's word. The one that says He will comfort us in our tribulations so that we can comfort those who are going through the same tribulation with the same comfort. (My paraphrase.) And I said to myself, "Thank you Lord for putting me in the right place, at the right time, with Your word in my heart." Rest assured, my friends, if you are in a "tribulation" God has already sent someone on your behalf!

*I*WAS LISTENING TO A NEW SONG ON A CD IN THE CAR AND COULD SEE THE TITLE on the display screen. It said, "Rent the Heavens". And I thought, that can't be right. How would that work? "Dear God.....I'm having this worship event and I was wondering if we could rent a spot in Heaven just for the night. I'd like a place big enough to hold maybe 200-300 people and, of course, as much of your glory as possible. The theme would be the greatness of Your majesty and splendor and if You could spare some angels to sing along with us, that would be awesome!" Obviously that was not the correct name of the song. It is actually, "Rend the Heavens" but apparently my computerized CD player did not understand the word rend and replaced it with rent. M-m-m. What a difference that one letter made. The difference between renting, which is to occupy or use for a short while or one day at a time, and rending which is to remove with force or pull apart.....to open. Renting Heaven would only give us a glimpse of His glory for a short time. On the other hand, if God were to rend the Heavens, the gates would be pulled apart and we would see in full the Glory and the Majesty of the Lord! Oh God, give us the passion and the desire to never stop crying out to You from here on earth with our worship, praise, and prayers until You rend the Heavens and we find ourselves fully lost in your glory, surrounded by your love, and, unlike renting, taking full possession of our place as children of the Most High King!! And, Lord, I would still love to have that choir of angels! I mean, seriously, the harmonies have got to be out of this world!!

*M*Y 19 MONTH OLD GRANDDAUGHTER LILY LOVES TO TALK WITH ME ON THE phone. When my son Matthew calls she somehow knows it's me and comes running to the phone to "talk". And apparently she knows what she's saying because Matthew says she becomes quite excited using facial expressions, hand movements and even pausing at appropriate times for me to respond. I honestly have no idea what she is saying but I love every minute of this exchange between us. The other night we were having a conversation and when it was time for her to go her daddy said, "Say bye-bye Grandma." I heard something that made no sense at all. He said it again and still nothing understandable. But the third time she loudly, lovingly, CLEARLY said, "Bye-bye Gamma!" Words cannot describe this feeling. She knows me and she called me by name! First I whispered, "She said Gamma!" I said it again a little louder and then I yelled downstairs to my husband, "Lily just called me Gamma!!" I don't care what kind of day you've had, that right there will make it all worth it! And it made me wonder how the Lord reacted the first time we called Him by name. I don't imagine He got as giddy about it as I did but I can picture Him elbowing whichever angel was closest to Him and saying, "Did you hear that? She just called me by name! She knows Me! And you know what? She may not always understand everything she's saying, but I do! I hear, I know, and I understand because I made the very heart that beats within her and created it with the desire to call Me by name! And she is worth it all to Me!" Thank you Lily Bean for calling me Gamma! Thank you Lord for calling me Your own!!

*L*ILY BEAN HAS A ROUTINE EVERY NIGHT WITH HER DADDY. WHEN HE GETS HOME from work she knows the first thing he does is get a snack, which is usually Cheez-it crackers or Pringles, and he always shares it with her. So when he comes in the door she gets herself in the "snack position" which is to sit on the floor with her little legs crossed and waits for him to begin the sharing! Well, this week Lily is not feeling so well. She has ear infections, a terrible cough, a fever and hasn't been eating well. When her daddy came home the other night she was napping. But somehow she heard him get his snack for the evening and got herself up and went right to his side. She climbed up into his lap and, although she did not feel like eating, she handed a snack to her daddy, and then snuggled into his lap and rested while he ate. How precious is that! It wasn't the snack she wanted, it was that special time with her daddy. And, friends, I know I use my granddaughter in a lot of my stories but her childlike ways remind me so much of how our relationship with our Father should be. Isn't the time we spend with Him more important than the gifts He has for us? Shouldn't we want to climb into the lap of our Father when we don't feel so good and seek comfort from the One who loves us so much? And shouldn't we always desire to give Him our love even when we don't feel so loveable ourselves? Yes, that's exactly the way it should be! Because He said, "Seek first the Kingdom of God and all these things will be added to you!" Which in Lily's case might just include Cheez-it's and Pringles! Let His love surround you and His comfort embrace you every single moment!

*L*AST NIGHT WE HAD OUR WEEKLY BIBLE STUDY. WE MEET IN THE CHAPEL WHERE there are tables and chairs and I was seated at a table with my husband and a friend. Like always, we started the meeting with prayer and assumed the proper position with heads bowed, eyes closed. When we were done praying I opened my eyes and saw a nice young man standing next to the empty chair where my husband had been when we started! He was a visitor and asked me if anybody was sitting in that chair. Most people would have just replied no, but as I've explained before, blondes take most questions quite literally and there WAS somebody in that chair just moments before. So my response went something like this: I looked at him, then at the empty chair, and then back at him and said, "Um.....I.....well........ ah". I briefly scanned the room, glanced under the table just to be sure, looked to my right to see if my friend was still there, and then back at the young man. The whole time I'm thinking, "Where did Larry go? No one else disappeared after prayer so I don't think he was raptured without the rest of us!" I finally managed to give him a better response by saying "Yes....I mean no.....I mean, please take this seat!!" Good grief! Figures the first time this young man comes to our church he seeks directions from the only blonde in the room!!! Now I'm thinking this poor guy is never going to come back when I remembered this verse from the Bible. "Do not forget to entertain strangers, for by so doing some have unwittingly entertained angels." (Hebrews 13:2) Ha! There you go!! Unwittingly...yes! Entertaining.....you betcha! Nailed it!!!

*I*BREW FRESH ICE TEA. I GENERALLY DRINK IT MORE THAN MY HUSBAND LARRY BUT for whatever reason he took a particular liking to the last pitcher I made. He actually drank most of it forcing me to hold the pitcher of ice (minus tea) in front of him and give him the look! You know the one. Raised eyebrows, steely eyes, and the word "REALLY??" forming on your lips! Which led us into a…..well…..a dispute. He said he didn't drink that much. I said he did. Dispute ended! A few days later I brewed a fresh pot and put it in the frig. We were both in the kitchen and I felt a little bad over what we now refer to as "the ice tea incident". So I said to him, "Larry, you CAN drink the ice tea in the frig." He turned to face me each of us raising one eyebrow. Our eyes locked, our bodies tensed and we held that position for about 5 seconds until he replied, "I know I can drink the tea in the frig. I'm not afraid of drinking the tea in the frig!" And then the raised eyebrows and set jaw turned into twinkling eyes and a smile as he finished his declaration with, "I'm afraid of you!" And as we both started to laugh I thought to myself, this is irrefutable proof that when mamma ain't happy, ain't nobody happy! And one simple comment just made this mamma happy! Take note gentlemen of Larry's intelligent reasoning and use of humor to successfully defuse what could have been a stand-off of epic proportion! You're a good man Larry Boog! You're a good man! Next pitcher's on me!!!

Jacqualine K. Boog

*L*AST NIGHT WAS MY WORST DRIVE HOME EVER! THE WHITE OUTS WERE SO INTENSE that in the bad spots I could see down the road less than half a mile. In the really bad spots I could only see 10-20 feet! I was white knuckling it all the way and then realized I was talking to myself. I was repeating over and over again, "Just don't stop! Just don't stop!" kind of like that fish Dory in "Finding Nemo" when she kept saying, "Just keep swimming". The desire to pull over and try and get out of the situation was overwhelming and the absolute worst thing I could do! I'd just be a sitting target for the guy coming up behind me. I would look straight into the mess and could see nothing but a curtain of white which made me lose my bearings. But if I kept my eyes on the road (where I could see it) and followed the path of those before me, I could manage to keep going at a slow and steady pace. When I finally got home and my heart rate had returned to normal, I thought about what lesson I could "see" in this. It made me think of times that I've felt like I was caught in a blinding emotional storm. Where I couldn't find my way and felt like the only thing to do was stop. Stop thinking about it. Stop trying to get through it. Stop trying to find my way out of it! But that would only leave me as a sitting target for the enemy. However, if I learn not to try and battle through in my own understanding, and keep my eyes and my feet (or wheels) on the path set before me, eventually the way becomes abundantly clear! Because that IS God's promise to us! So maybe what Dory and I should learn to say is, "Just keep trusting! Just keep trusting!" and keep our feet (or fins) on the path of Him who has gone before us. Because the One who's leading is the same One who made the way!

*M*Y HUSBAND LARRY AND I RECENTLY EXPERIENCED A BIT OF A SETBACK FORCING us to make some decisions that we thought we wouldn't have to deal with for at least a few more years. So, after a couple of days of thinking about everything, we decided we needed to de-stress a little and took a day trip to my happy place…..."Jackie's World". 'Cause every one knows I'm the queen there and I needed to wear the royal crown for awhile! We took some great photos of the ice formations along the lake shore. I sent a photo of one of the massive ice mountains to our pastor who I knew was praying for us. His response was this, "It's good to get away and see the bigger picture (no pun intended) but there's truth to it." I got to thinking about his comment. The picture was beautiful but all you could see was the "mountain". What you couldn't see was the beautiful lake behind it, the massive Mighty Mac to the left, the horizon filtered in yellows to the right, or the rest of the people there oohing and aahing over this phenomenon of nature. How often in life do we get caught up in only seeing the mountain and not what else is really in the picture? We focus on the massive problem and fail to see the answers that surround it. Like the beauty that is hidden just on the other side, the "bridge" God has provided to get us from this closed door to the new one He will open, the incredible answer that is just beyond the horizon filtered through His hands, and all the friends who are standing by supporting you, loving you, and cheering you on with their ooh's and aah's of God's awesome power! So, I've decided to not focus on the mountain in front of me. I'm going to take my pastor's advice and see the "bigger picture"! I have also decided I will wear the royal crown a little longer. Because, well, if the crown fits……..!

*T*HE GIRLS AT WORK HAVE DISCOVERED THAT IT'S QUITE EASY TO STARTLE ME. AND there's an entertainment value that comes with it as I tend to flail my arms about, make funny faces, and occasionally my feet will get in on the act and make me look like I'm running but getting nowhere! And now I'm convinced they lie in wait for an opportunity to sneak up on me. Well, a few days ago I inadvertently played the sneaky part. Some of you may remember that I have a young friend that is 6'9" tall (and still growing) and plays drums with our worship team once in awhile. He's usually at college but this weekend he was home for Easter and joined us on drums. After the team finished our practice a young lady was warming up on a song she was doing for a special. Zach was in the back of the sanctuary listening and I went back to ask him a question. He was sitting in a chair, eyes closed, drumming on his legs, on the chair, on pretty much anything he could find to drum on. (Drummers do that. It's how they stay on their A game! Plus they can't sit still!) So I lightly tapped him on the shoulder. He came unglued! He jumped, then leaned away from me putting his hands up to shield himself like he thought I was going to smack him! Seriously?? Standing beside him I was still shorter than he was sitting down!! He said, "Jackie, you scared me!" I said, "I know and it was pretty funny!" So what did I learn from this? I think it's much funnier to scare a 6'9" young man than to scare a 5'3" old(er) lady! You know why? Because the 6'9" young man gets more air when he jumps!!! Bahahahahahaha!!!!!!!

WE WERE AT OUR SON'S HOUSE LAST WEEK CELEBRATING OUR GRANDDAUGHTER Brynn's 10th birthday. My 14 year old grandson Elliott, who is 5'11" tall, asked me if I wanted to shoot some hoops with him. Clearly he was oblivious to the fact that I'm only 5'3", almost 62, and it was raining! However, one should never, ever say no when your teenage grandchild asks you to do something with them. They are already convinced we are not very cool! Let's not add fuel to that fire! So I put on my jacket and out into the drizzle we went. I laid down the rules. He did all the chasing of stray balls and anything that hit nearby cars was his fault! I took my place and dribbled a couple of times just to make it look like I knew what I was doing. (The basketball! I was not drooling!) My first shot was nothing but net! No, really!! That's all I hit was the net…about 6 inches under the rim! My next attempt was granny style, two handed from between the knees! That one missed entirely falling short about 1 foot in front of the basket. Elliott, on the other hand, was putting them in left and right even rebounding a few! Show off!! I finally said I was ready to go inside. Elliott said, "Grandma, you can't go in until you make a basket!" Wait!! What?? That was NOT in the original game plan. Okay. This was it. I was confident I could do this. I steadied myself, raised the ball up and calculated my shot. I could almost hear the Rocky theme song running through my mind! A little bend in the elbows, a tiny jump, and I let it go off my fingertips and straight into the basket!! Boom!! I'm not sure Elliott fully appreciated my victory dance but I was rocking it!! I scored this basket for all the rest of the cool grandparents out there. You know who you are! And you're welcome!!

*I*HAVE A SMALL COLLECTION OF FIGURINES CALLED "SNOW BABIES". THEY ARE LITTLE snow angels dressed in snowsuits with tiny angel wings. One of them is a delightful little cherub called "Rejoice". She stands with her arms high in the air holding a golden staff of music going from hand to hand over her head. She recently had a little accident and broke her arm. It is completely disconnected from her body and yet it remains in the same place. It is not on the ground next to her. It is not hanging at her side. It is still high in the air clinging to her banner of joy! And that's the thing…her gold strand of music is holding her arm securely in place until it is mended. Which is taking some time because apparently the right choice of glue is a very precise decision and requires weeks of formulated theories and research. My husband is currently working on that project. Who knew? I would have just slapped some Elmer's on it! But that's not my point. How many times have you felt like you are broken and being held together by a strand? Do you remember God's word to us? The one that says He will rejoice over us with singing! His song of joy is exactly what is holding my little angel together! So the next time you feel like you can't even lift a finger, be brave and lift all ten of them straight toward Heaven and grab hold of even just a portion of that banner of love He sings over you. I guarantee there is absolutely nothing that can break you away from Him and His love song!

ONE OF MY HIGH SCHOOL CLASSMATES HAD A BIT OF A SITUATION RECENTLY. SHE posted a screenshot of her phone which showed the temperature as 22 degrees.......in Florida!! Unlikely but...hey...it was her smart phone! It couldn't be wrong....right?? Her daughter saw the post and pointed out to her mom and to all the rest of us that she had somehow set her phone to Celsius. Oops!! My friend had what is referred to as a "blonde moment" and reached out to me to see if I could put some kind of spiritual spin on it to help her out. I'm not sure if that's because I'm blonde or spiritual! Doesn't matter! Challenge accepted! So I thought about it, and thought about it, and thought about it some more. And decided there's no getting around it! This was, in fact, a "blonde moment"! Pure and simple! However, and I'm not saying this is a word from the Lord, but I kind of felt like He might have said, "I made the sun and the moon and the stars in the sky! I can make it hot where it should be cold and cold where it should be hot! But you, my dear child, will have to learn the difference between Celsius and Fahrenheit on your own!" Boom! (That wasn't the expression "boom". That was a clap of thunder. He was making a point!) So, there you go my friend. This one's for you and for every blonde who is not as smart as her phone!!!

A FEW NIGHTS AGO MY HUSBAND LARRY KNOCKED OVER MY AFRICAN VIOLET. I heard the commotion and went to see what happened. Larry was standing there next to the spot where my plant used to be. I told him to just leave it but he insisted on helping. What I saw next is a bit difficult to explain. It was kind of like when the super hero begins fighting in a movie and everything goes to slow motion. To begin with Larry totally disappeared from my sight beside the dining room table. I guess he bent down to pick up my plant. The next thing I see is one of his arms coming up from somewhere and kind of grasping for a chair and totally missing. Then his arm went down and a leg appeared. And finally I see the rest of him slowly fall into the back of the recliner which sort of gave with his impact and I thought I heard him cuss but I must have been mistaken because Larry never cusses! I stood there watching this procession of arms and legs rolling across the floor and when he finally landed asked, "What did you hurt??" "My head", he replied. I said, "On what? The back of the recliner is soft?" He said, "Yes, yes it is, except for this wooden slat just to the left of center!" Hence the cussing sound which I obviously misunderstood because Larry never cusses!! He got up and pulled himself together and sat in his recliner. (On the seat rather than sprawled across the back of it!) I cleaned up the mess and then inquired as to his injuries. "Is your head okay?" He replied, "Yes. But I'm not sure which one of you to answer! How long has there been three of you!!" His funny bone was obviously unharmed!! Just an average night in "Jackie's World"! Ask Larry. He'll tell you! He falls head over heels in love with me over and over again!

*L*ARRY AND I ARE A BLENDED FAMILY. HE IS NOT THE BIOLOGICAL FATHER OF MY children. They were never legally adopted and so the boys and their children have a different last name than we have. But there was an adoption that took place. Not on paper but in the hearts of Larry and his family. No questions asked, no papers to sign, only acceptance as if they were blood born into the Boog family. And at each gathering, every holiday, every birthday, they are treated as if they have always been a part of this family. They have aunts and uncles, lots of cousins, and a loving grandmother and great-grandmother who all love them as their own. And, of course, there's the brave man who married me and became a father to my children! I can never explain how valuable this is. To know you are accepted. To know you belong. To know you are loved. There is another family that has this same kind of love. It's called the family of God. And when we say yes to His invitation to become His child, we are immediately adopted and become part of His family. Not an adoption on legal paper but written in His book and kept in His heart. We become joint heirs with His Son Jesus, sharing in His name. And the same love bestowed on Him now belongs to us! Signed and sealed with the blood of the Lamb! Do you know how valuable that is? Do you know you belong? Do you know you are loved? Well, you should! I know of no better definition of what a family should be! And to those of you out there who took on someone else's family as your own...thank you! You did something extraordinary and beautiful!

*O*N OUR RECENT TRIP UP NORTH WE BABYSAT OUR GRANDDAUGHTER LILY BEAN while her mom and dad went to a movie. We decided to take her to the hotel pool. Now folks, let me stop right her and say on my behalf, I raised boys. A swimsuit was basically a pair of shorts that tied in the front. Lily's suit was a one piece ballerina tutu with spaghetti straps that crossed in the back. Matthew had warned me it was a bit of a challenge to get on. Really?? It should have come with an instruction manual and a numbered picture guide! My first attempt was to have her step into it. Seemed simple enough. One foot in each leg hole, pull it up, and put her arms into the straps. And there she stood before me…with both straps wrapped securely around JUST her right arm and shoulder! So I tried laying her on the floor and sort of "schooching" the suit on her thinking I would have more control of the straps. I stood her up and there she was as before, both straps wrapped only on the right! At this point grandpa offered to help. I cannot describe the look I gave him! I don't know what I did different on my third try but all of a sudden she was standing before me in a pink ballerina tutu with spaghetti straps crossed in the back! We looked at each other and smiled! (I had been talking to her through the whole process so she wouldn't think Grandma had lost it but I may have missed that boat some time ago!) We headed down to the pool and Grandpa took the lead in the water. After a few minutes I asked Lily, "Are you swimming?" She said, "Ya!" "Are you having fun?" "Ya!" "Are you cold?" "Ya!" "Do you want to get out?" "Ya!" TWENTY minutes getting that swimsuit on and FIVE minutes in the water. But she was rocking that suit with every strap in place! Grandma….. one! Pink ballerina tutu swimsuit with spaghetti straps…..zero! Boom!!

O UR SWEET LITTLE 2 YEAR OLD GRANDDAUGHTER IS AN ADELE WANNA-BE! AND her favorite song is "Hello". Lily Bean sings it as only she can, with her whole heart! Her parents recently sent me a video of Lily watching Adele sing "Hello" on Youtube. Lily sits in complete admiration of this artist singing along with her like she's on stage! When she gets to the chorus of the song, "Hello from the other side" Lily lets it fly! (You seriously can't sing Adele unless you belt it!!) And I think The Bean has a whole octave on Adele because she hits a note that might possibly have the capacity to break glass!! Lily copies Adele's every move, she tries to sing each word, she scrunches up her little face like she's singing the blues, and then there's that high note that is truly indescribable! At the very end of the video Lily sits in complete silence for just a second waiting to see if Adele is done and when she's satisfied the song is over she puts her little hands together, applauds this fine artist, and shouts, "Yea!!!!". So I'm wondering…..is it possible we could sit in complete adoration of our Lord and worship Him like we are in the Throne Room? Could we try and match His every word, meet His every move, sing His song with all our heart? (Well, minus the sound that might possibly break glass. Although the Lord does enjoy a truly joyful sound!) And when He does something beautiful, like He does every day, could we watch in awe and wonder enthusiastically applauding our Lord and shouting, "Yea God!!" Yes! I believe we can! If we are a Jesus wanna-be!!!

WE HAD LUNCH A FEW WEEKS AGO WITH SOME FRIENDS WHO WISH TO REMAIN anonymous. Actually, after the conversation we had, they wish to not admit they know me!! It all began when I asked about a baby horse. An innocent enough question regarding the wellbeing of said horse. Which began an entire seminar on the names and genders of various farm animals. For instance, did you know that all baby horses are foals, but a male is a colt and a female is a filly? However, much to my surprise, a pony is NEVER a baby horse!! What?? Hold on!! Then what is it?? According to those in the know it's a breed all it's own. They are simply ponies and various kinds at that! But that was just the beginning! I learned that not all cows are cows! A female is a cow, a male is a bull. Collectively they are cattle! And among the horses and cattle there are geldings and steers. I am too much of a lady to tell you what happened to them to change their status! The next animal we took on was donkeys. They are not related to horses except by marriage which brings us to……the mule! He (or she…..I'm not even going to go there!) is the "child" of a female horse and a male donkey!! (And no one thought to call him a horskey???) MIND! BLOWN! My friends decided to stop the "down on the farm" lesson at this point because when they went into the donkey story I went into the deer in the headlights look! I guess it all just proves the point that you can lead a horse to water, but if the foals, the cattle, the donkey and the mule all show up there won't be much left to drink!!! ☺

WE HAVE A BATHROOM SINK THAT DOESN'T DRAIN PROPERLY AND IT WAS REALLY irritating me! I was leaving for the grocery store and gave Larry instructions to please do something about it. (It's possible I did NOT use the word please!) When I got back he informed me he was able to fix it but he had to remove all my stuff on the top shelf of the bathroom cupboard to get to it. I gave him "the look" (you know the one) and said, "ALL my stuff??" I should explain that I have a tendency (okay…it's a full blown addiction) to collect a LOT of bath, body and hair products which I keep in that cupboard. I should also mention I have a tendency (okay….it's full blown OCD) to be very organized! The thought of all my "stuff" being out of order about put me over the edge. Larry could see I was coming unglued and said, "It's okay. I'll put it back." I told him to forget it. I would do it. (Again, those may not have been my exact words.) So I finished up in the kitchen and went upstairs to put my "stuff" away. To my surprise, every bottle was taken care of and perfectly in place! I asked Larry what happened. He said he took care of them. I then asked the obvious question, "But how did you get them exactly where they were before??" His answer? "When I took them out I placed them in the same position on the floor so I could put them back the way you had them." Now I ask you…how much more thoughtful could one man be? Thoughtful enough to understand my quirky obsessions!! And smart enough to know he has to live with me! And to answer the question that's on everyone's mind…..6 rows, 3 deep, everything facing front, cleansers first, lotions behind, hair products to the left. Please don't think I'm weird! Well….you know….anymore than usual!!! It's not always easy "Living in Jackie's World"!

*I*HAD THE PRIVILEGE OF WATCHING A FRIEND OF MINE SKYDIVE FOR HER BIRTHDAY. It was an incredible sight. And she made it look so easy! She went up in the plane, jumped out the door (with a buddy coach), floated effortlessly to the ground and landed like a pro! As we were all applauding her magnificent feat I heard someone murmur, "He lost his chute!" referring to her buddy coach. The crowd that had gathered continued to talk about it. And I thought, "What do you mean he lost his chute!! I just saw them safely land......with a chute!!" I kept hearing people kind of whispering about it and it occurred to me that maybe it was the spare chute. I mean they have to have an extra in case the first one doesn't open, right? And then I heard someone say, "Found it! It was still on the plane!" What!! He left the spare chute on the plane!! Then I looked and realized the man was holding a SHOE!! Not a CHUTE....a SHOE! For Heaven's sake people enunciate!!! When you're on an airfield and you've just watched a good friend jump from an airplane there is a HUGE.....HUGE difference between a chute and a shoe!! A shoe you can land without. A chute...not so much! In the event you are in a similar situation try to be mindful of the fact that some in your group my have slightly decreased hearing, or be prone to misunderstanding, or could be blonde!!! So, please, for the sake of hearing impaired, misunderstood blondes everywhere, enunciate your words! And congratulations to my friend! Your "shoe" unfurled beautifully!!!

$\mathcal{P}$ASTOR MIKE AND I DID AN AFTERNOON CHURCH SERVICE FOR OUR LOCAL ASSISTED living. We had a delightful group of saints eager to sing their favorite songs. One gentleman in particular, who had a very nice booming voice, seemed to be the leader of the pack. He chose the first song, "I'll Fly Away". I started playing and he jumped right in. Beautiful voice, in tune, but a beat and a half behind me! The lady next to him was kind of waving her arms up and down. Couldn't tell for sure if she was trying to speed me up, slow him down, or was actually "flying away"! And on the other side of the man was a lady who elbowed him, scowled, and pointed at me. He scowled right back at her and kept going. For a minute it kind of looked like an old vaudeville show! And Mike and I were having problems of our own. I was having trouble seeing my music (dim lighting) and he was having trouble reaching the high notes (I don't know his excuse) and, all in all, we've had better moments! But we forged on doing the best we could. And then we suddenly found ourselves in a perfect song where I could actually see the music (with minimal squinting), that wasn't too high (with minimal squeaking), and that everyone seemed to know. The elderly gentleman led us all in crisp, clear tones and totally on the beat! The song was "Open My Eyes That I May See" and the Lord allowed me a view I had not anticipated. He opened my eyes to see a lady who maybe used to direct a choir. He showed me a gentleman that possibly was the lead in a men's quartet. He revealed to me a lady that perhaps was a section leader and had to throw an elbow or two to keep her group in line! Thank you Father for allowing me just a glimpse of precious memories from times that might have been. And for reminding me that it's not perfection You seek, but the sound that comes from a joyful heart!

*M*Y REFRIGERATOR, FOR WHATEVER REASON, MAKES AN OVERABUNDANCE OF ICE, sometimes actually spilling over the edge of the bin. I guess it doesn't realize it's still full! And when you want ice, it won't give it up without a battle. First it drops just a few into your cup to tease you. Then it makes a little snow and several little chips of ice which usually end up on the floor practically invisible to the eye but found very easily by the naked foot! Next the freezer trembles a little, kind of like it's having a small seizure. Then it rumbles and rattles a bit and finally spews about 150 ice cubes from the chute. (Okay, that's exaggerating. It's probably only 145!) At this point, I begin to look like I'm playing some kind of party game as I balance my cup full of ice in one hand while trying to catch and fling ice across the room into the sink with the other! I've actually become quite proficient at this missing the sink only on rare occasions! And as an added perk cleaning up the mess has become a daily exercise routine! The whole thing has given new meaning to the phrase "my cup runneth over!" But what if it was a spiritual cup running over? What if there was a tremble, a sound like thunder, and the Lord opened the flood gates of Heaven and your cup was suddenly pressed down, shaken together, running over with abundant blessings from above?? Would you shake your fist and complain about the mess that was made? Or would you fold your hands in gratitude and thank the Lord that you are no longer the mess you once were!! The repairman will be here in about two weeks and will hopefully fix my overactive ice maker. The Lord has always been here "fixing" my life over and over again, reminding me how very full I am.....even spilling over with the goodness of God!

I LIKE LONG-ISH CARDIGAN STYLE SWEATERS. THEY ARE A STAPLE IN MY WARDROBE and I'll tell you why. They hide a "multitude of sins" creating a slimming effect! I went for a walk the other night and threw on one of my sweaters. But it turned out to be much hotter and more humid than I anticipated. So I had no choice but to remove my sweater because as good as the cardigan look was; the red faced, sweaty look….not so much!! I didn't want to carry it so I hung it over my shoulders. But this gave me a matronly lady look. Not what I was going for. So then I tied it around my waist. Nice! Kind of preppy, kind of sporty! I held my head high and walked on. Until I reached downtown and the first store front with a large window. I glanced to the side wanting to see if I looked as stylish as I thought I did. Much to my surprise, the sweater was no longer "slimming" and the "effect" was to create a much larger behind than I thought I had! Apparently, store windows have the same problem as cameras. They add at least 10 lbs!!! I was committed now as I was too hot to put it back on so I continued my walk with a large load following me! Which makes me ask this question. How often do we look in the mirror and not like what we see. Physically? Emotionally? Even spiritually? And we walk around thinking we are hiding our excess baggage beneath outer garments. Well, God has a better plan. In fact, He has a better garment! The garment of praise! And unlike my long-ish sweater it does not just hide a multitude of sins, it replaces the spirit of heaviness removing excess baggage and large loads! Now, I'm not going to get rid of my sweaters because there are some things that are okay to try and hide. However, the next time I am dealing with "heaviness", it's the garment of praise I will choose!!

*D*ID YOU KNOW THERE ARE FEW THINGS MORE PLEASING TO A MOTHER THAN having all her children gathered around her table eating their favorite foods? I get so caught up in being with them that I lose my own desire to eat. I just want to enjoy their fellowship! Each moment is special. Like my son Michael giving me a hard time because I forgot his favorite cheese ball! (Seriously! Did not know it meant that much to you!) Tami, Jen, and Murp discussing who's the favorite daughter-in-law based on which son they married! Our twins, Mark and Matthew, going into what could be a standup comic routine that leaves us all in fits of laughter! And watching our 5 foot 11 inch grandson Elliott get down on the floor and help his two year old cousin Lily color. Our granddaughters Brynn and Ariel gathering all the special toys that belong only at Grandma's and forming their own little circle to play. They are laughing, their eyes sparkle, and they are enjoying family time and the feast set before them! Did you know there is another banquet table being made ready for us laden with all of our favorite things found only in His house? And the Lord is at the head of this table waiting and watching for His children to arrive. And when they do, the great feast will begin and God will rejoice in the love and fellowship now bringing His children together. We will be caught up in His smiles, His laughter, His love. And we will lose all desire for anything except to fellowship with him. Now, I have to admit, I almost didn't post this story. Because I couldn't find a proper ending. But then I realized, it really has no ending. As a matter of fact, when it appears it's coming to an end it will truly be just the beginning! So, as they say my friends….live, laugh, love! And remember that the best family feast is yet to come!!!

WE HAD A WONDERFUL WORSHIP SERVICE SUNDAY MORNING. LOTS OF PRAISE, banners, shouts of joy, and even a little Spirit led dancing! After the service I went to the office as I usually do to take care of music. I keep mine in a book and as I opened it to pull the music out a huge, black pincher bug came running out of the pocket in the front! (I seriously just stopped typing and made little pinching motions with my fingers!!) It ran out of and under my book, back through the pages, slipped underneath a page or two and then came running back out, always in a zigzag fashion. Probably had military training! I thought about squishing it when it ran under a page but who wants bug guts all over their music?? At some point I might have jumped and squealed a little. No one heard me. I called for one of the deacons who were in the other office taking care of the morning's offerings. They ignored me! I think I might have even shouted to the Lord Himself fully expecting a lightning bolt to come from the sky and smite the little bugger! But that probably would have been over kill (ha!) and could have scorched the counter top! (I'm sure God thought of that before rescuing me in that manner!) It finally ran into a crack between the counter tops and was gone. If all this wasn't bad enough it suddenly dawned on me that the bug had come with me to church in MY book which had been laying on MY bedroom floor beside MY bed!!! Ya....I'm gonna think about that for awhile! However, in spite of this ordeal it could have been worse. That thing could have come running out of my book while I was playing and singing during worship! At which point my congregation would have witnessed a whole new level to "dancing in the Spirit" complete with shouting! Although it would not have been of the joyful nature! I'm just sayin'.....

A FEW WEEKS AGO AT OUR WEDNESDAY NIGHT BIBLE STUDY WE BEGAN LIKE always, with prayer. Pastor Mike said he would start and encouraged us to pray out as we felt led for the needs that were mentioned. He began to pray and what followed next was........the dreaded awkward silence. The next thing I hear is Mike saying, "Okay STOP!!. Now I'll admit it startled me a little bit because, and I'm not proud of this, I think I had nodded off. And I thought was I dreaming? Had we moved passed prayer and I missed it? Was there some kind of unwritten 5 second rule (like when you drop food on the floor) between when one person stops praying and the next starts?? No! No! And most definitely no!! So what did happen? Well, I think we start to question the gifts God has already given us and we ask am I good enough to do this? Will I say the right words? Will God understand my feeble attempt to express my heart? Yes! Yes! And most definitely yes!! Because God knows. God understands and all it takes is the mention of His name. So the next time you're asked to pray, stand up and let your voice be heard! Even if all you can get out is, "Lord, please be with (fill in the name) because they need your help!" Trust me!...whether you pray with the eloquence of a sage prayer warrior or the innocence of a child, your prayer is still heard in His heart! All this being said, I would make sure that you do not allow too much time to pass between when the person before you stops and you start. Because, honestly, I'm not really clear on that 5 second rule thing!

A FEW DAYS AGO I WAS WOUNDED AT WORK. I WAS STACKING A BUNCH OF PAPERS and they slid between my first and second fingers and….PAPER CUT!!! There is no way to put a band-aid between your fingers with any effectiveness. I've heard you can use super glue. Um….no thank you! And properly sanitizing your hands is out of the question or worse yet, forgetting about the cut, sanitizing your hands and being totally unprepared for what comes next!! (Most of the ladies just said, "E-e-w-w-w!" A few men actually fainted!) And this kind of wound comes from something that seems so harmless…like paper! I think from time to time we all suffer wounds from seemingly harmless things. And we end up with small cuts of bitterness, little wounds of unforgiveness, tiny tears in relationships. They seem like nothing and we kind of forget about them until they are stirred up by life and we are totally unprepared for what comes next as we relive the very thing that caused the small wound and begin to hurt all over again. So what is the most effective healing for these wounds? Well, super glue is probably not an option. But a super power is! The love of Jesus liberally applied to each tiny root of bitterness, every hurt from unforgiveness, and every relationship that needs mending. And unlike a band-aid which only covers the problem, this remedy seeps deep down into the hurt and heals from the inside out! Also, it feels way better than hand sanitizer on a paper cut!! (Most of the ladies just said "Good word!" But some of the men just came to, read the rest of this post, and passed out again!)

WE WENT TO GAYLORD SATURDAY AND MADE A STOP AT BATH AND BODY Works. (Like I wouldn't? Everybody knows I hold the market on their products!) They had a young man working the checkout counter who was extremely efficient. He used all of my coupons, made at least $40.00 of products come down to $23.00, AND…he managed to get 6 pump hand soaps, 2 bath products, and 5 little hand sanitizers into 1 itty bitty bag! I said, "Dude, (I like to use that word because it makes me seem younger) you really packed them in there!" And apparently feeling quite pleased with himself replied, "Yep! I did and you're welcome!" So I walked out of the store with my 10 lbs worth of items in a bag that was clearly meant to hold no more than 5 convinced it was going to fall through the bottom and hit the pavement before I got to the car! On the drive home I was thinking about this. The "object lesson" made me realize how much stress and worry I carry around in a heart that was clearly not meant to hold such a load. The Lord said, "Come to Me, all you who labor and are heavy laden, and I will give you rest. For My yoke is easy and My burden is light." And you can be absolutely confident that anything you give to Him will be completely safe and will never fall through His hands to the ground. He's got it! So, while my Bath and Body Works bag did hold up to the weight it was carrying, I think I'll put the "weight of the world" in the hands of the One who was meant to carry it. Okay then! Now that I've released that burden it's time to enjoy my new bath products!!

*S*UNDAY MORNING AS PASTOR MIKE DID HIS USUAL GREETING HE WAS GIVING A word of encouragement to those who might be struggling with troubles. But he got his words kind of mixed together and it came out as "strubbles"!! Which led one member of the worship team to sing the first line of "Nobody knows the strubbles I've seen!" (Hey….I tried not to but I just couldn't help myself!) and prompted our guitar player to suggest "Bridge over strubbled waters" . (Musicians have an unusual sense of humor!) But the truth is we all have strubbles. In the past week I have found some in my world. Generally they are not allowed in Jackie's World but occasionally a few slip through. And then it hit me. The last several posts I've done have had to do with letting the Lord carry our burdens; being able to let go of unforgiveness and bitterness; making sure we are on the path He has set before us. Wow! I write these things but can I live them? They look so good on paper but sometimes it's hard to get them in your heart. I've obviously said it before and now I'm going to say it again… He is the only path to rest and peace; the only One who can hold your world (and everybody else's) in His hands. So now it's time to listen to my own words and let myself be carried in His arms of love. And, quite honestly, that's the only way to be strubble free!!

Jacqualine K. Boog

_L_AST SUNDAY MORNING WAS A BEAUTIFUL WORSHIP SERVICE OVERFLOWING WITH the affirmation of God's love. When we came to altar time, my pastor felt led to invite me to come down for prayer. There was, however, one minor glitch. As I left the platform he asked my guitar players to continue singing the song we had been doing. Now these guys are amazing musicians and have beautiful voices. That being said, they had been singing harmony to my lead and when I walked away, continued to do so without anybody singing the melody. Which kind of reminds me of an Oreo cookie without the filling! (Get it? Cause the harmonies go around the melody! Ha!) And, on top of that, we were doing the song in my key (alto) which made it uncomfortable at best for these tenors to take the lead. But this team has always been obedient to what's asked of them. (Well, most of the time. On occasion they have failed to follow my directions and gone their own way. But there is really nothing you can do when a drummer decides to take charge!) And they were now determined to follow what pastor required. Here's what the Lord says about this. "Behold, to obey is better than sacrifice, and to heed than the fat of rams." (Um.....the latter part has nothing to do with the girth of my guitar players!) There are times when we are called to be obedient. It may not be comfortable, it could take us out of our "range" but hopefully we'll end up going His way and not our own. So, this may not have been their finest moment by worldly standards but in the heavenly realms they were shining stars and very pleasing to the Lord!

*T*HE NIGHT BEFORE THANKSGIVING I WAS DOING MY DINNER PREP AND WAS TRYING to figure out how long I needed to bake the ham. Larry came into the kitchen and I said, "8.85 lbs is almost a one lb ham, right?" He was disturbingly quiet. I asked the same question again and still no sound from him. So, rather than ask again I turned to him, eyebrows raised, and he's staring at me with an odd expression on his face. Now let me just add, in my mind I thought I had asked him if .85 was almost one pound. And, honestly, as long as we've been together I kind of assumed he spoke fluent blonde-ese! I mean, he's been my interpreter on many occasions. Obviously I was wrong because this one stumped him! I continued to stare at his bewildered face and he continued to stare at mine patiently waiting for me to process my own question. (Some days that can be a long wait!) When the proverbial light bulb finally blinked on, he breathed a sigh of relief. I think he was dreading trying to answer my question because, really, any answer was probably going to upset me. And he showed amazing restraint in waiting it out! (I've had a lot on my mind lately. I think he was concerned he might push me over the edge!) Do I have a great ending to this story? Not really. Other than 8.85 lbs is almost a NINE lb ham. Is there a spiritual application? I'm going to go with "Husbands love your wives" and leave it at that! And finally, can a blonde bake an 8.85 lb ham? To perfection!!

I WANTED TO WRITE A CHRISTMAS POST BUT COULDN'T GET OUT OF MY HEAD WHAT I heard in Walmart last night. There was an announcement that came over the main speaker saying, "Would the lady who was looking for her lima beans please come to the front desk." (Really? I would rather they stay lost!) But the thing is, this lady had lost something and if she followed the directions given to her, the item would soon be found! (Again….lima beans?) So, I know you're all wondering how I can turn this lima bean story into a Christmas message. Well….here goes! A very long time ago there were those who were lost and they were given directions as to finding what they were seeking. "Would those looking for the Child in a manger please come to Bethlehem. Would those looking for the King of Kings please follow the star in the East. Would all those seeking please knock and the door shall be opened to you. Are you in need of a Savior? Come and be found in Him!" It's a simple process really. Just follow the directions and the lost will always be found! So, there you go! Merry Christmas my friends! And may you "find" all you need in the Christ child, the King of Kings, the Savior born for us all Who came to seek and find the lost!

I HAD A CONVERSATION ON SPEAKER PHONE WITH MY SON MATTHEW AND 2 ½ YEAR old granddaughter Lily that went a little something like this:

Matthew: "Lily….Gramma's on the phone. You want to say hi?"

Lily: "Hi Papa!"

Papa: "Hi Lily!"

Matthew: "Don't forget Gramma!"

Lily: "Hi Papa!"

Matthew: "Lily….say hi to Gramma too!"

Lily: Unintelligible chatter ending with "Gramma" and followed by…"But I love my Papa!"

Matthew and Jen: "Bahahahahahahaha!!"

Disgruntled Gramma: "Are you kidding me??"

Matthew: "Tell Gramma bye."

Lily: "Bye Papa!"

Gramma: No words……just shaking head and rolling eyes!

About 40 minutes later when we arrive at their house:

Lily as she sees us coming in the door: "Daddy, Daddy, Gramma's here! Gramma's here!"

Boom!! She just needed to see my smiling face! First! Before Papa! Okay…I may have slammed the door in his face a little when we came in but…. hey….don't judge! I had a reputation to uphold for Gramma's everywhere!!

We went to visit Lily Bean the other night. She was so excited to see us that she began to chatter away with her pacifier in her mouth and wasn't making a lot of sense. Her mamma told her to take it out of her mouth and in her excitement she threw it towards her daddy and it landed somewhere behind the couch. Now this created a bit of a predicament as she has a strong attachment to her pacifier, especially at night, and their couch is very difficult to move. But Lily seemed not at all alarmed by the whole incident. She just stood there looking at her daddy. He called her up on the couch with him and they both leaned over the edge and spotted her pacifier. He asked if she could see it. She replied yes. He asked did she think she could get it. She answered yes. He then picked her up by her ankles and slowly lowered her behind the couch as I stood there watching like a deer caught in the headlights until all I could see of my granddaughter was the bottoms of her feet!! He said, "Have you got it?" She said, "Ya…I got it!" and he carefully pulled her back up until she landed safely in his lap pacifier firmly stuck between her lips! She was never worried. She had no fear. She listened to her daddy's voice and knew he had a firm grip on her. Guess we could all learn a lesson from Lily Bean. I'm thinking the next time I'm in a "predicament", I'm going to listen to my Father's voice, trust completely that He has a firm grip on me, (although I would like to believe He has me by the hands and not dangling by my feet), and I'll end up sitting safely in His lap! (Probably without the pacifier!) My son Matthew actually suggested I tell this story on Facebook. And….. so I did. And now he's going to say, "Mom, you "Jesus-ized" my daughter's story!" And I'll say, "Mmmmm…so I did!" ☺

*A*FTER LIVING MANY YEARS IN AN AREA SURROUNDED BY THE GREAT LAKES, I have noticed something about the water in the colder months. As the temperatures begin to chill the water becomes sluggish almost appearing to be heavy. When the wind kicks up even the waves seem to roll at a slower pace. And in a very hard winter, as ice begins to form around the edges and over the top, the water seems to stop moving completely. While this may paint a pretty picture I found myself comparing it to how it is when our love of the Lord grows cold. We become sluggish in our efforts to study His word. When the winds of the Spirit kick up we move but at a slower pace. And in the very hard times of our lives we can let the cold settle around our hearts and seem to stop moving completely in our efforts to find Him. Unlike the lake caught in winter's cold, we don't have to wait for warmer weather to be thawed out. And it only takes a few simple things to chip away that ice from our hearts. Surrender...to the heart of the Father. Obedience...to the call of His word. Passion...for His Holy presence. That's it! However, in the other scenario you'll need a little more. I suggest a coat, boots, hat, scarf, mittens, hand warmers, feet warmers, and...your camera. Because it really does paint a beautiful picture. As will you when you allow the warmth of the Son to shine in your life!

Jacqualine K. Boog

WE WERE VISITING WITH OUR GRANDDAUGHTER LILY A FEW WEEKS AGO. (SEEMS like I start a lot of my posts with this same comment! But, it is what it is!) When we were ready to leave she was saying her usual goodbyes which included the following, "Bye Gamma, bye Papa, I love you!" But this night she added a little something extra. "Thank you for me! And… you're welcome!!" What? Now there's a girl with a solid sense of self worth and obviously thinking we should all be aware of that. But maybe in her child's mind what she was really trying to express was thank you for her life. "Thank you for my mamma and daddy and family that love me! Thank you for my Klip Klop Castle and the new fish in my aquarium! Thank you for my cute smile and infectious laugh! And most of all…thank you for me!" And I find myself once again learning a valuable lesson from this little one. Because we should all have that same sense of self worth in the One who created us. After all, He knew us before we were even formed in our mother's womb. He is aware of every hair on our heads, (or lack thereof) and we are each uniquely created in His image. So the next time I get down on my knees, I'm going to thank the Lord for a family that loves me, for the gifts He daily gives, for my crooked smile and quirky sense of humor, and most of all, for who I am in Him! Thank you Lord for me!! And for those of you who know me well…you're welcome!!!

$\mathcal{A}$T ONE OF OUR RECENT FAMILY GATHERINGS, MY GRANDDAUGHTER LILY WAS AT the table with us and somebody asked her to smile. She lit up the room with a beautiful, yet slightly crooked smile. And I thought to myself, "That looks strangely familiar." It wasn't long before I realized it was the same smile I saw many times on her daddy's face, my middle child Matthew. (And yes, I know that he and his brother are identical twins but Matthew was born five minutes before Mark and five minutes when you're giving birth to twins is huge….HUGE!) I so loved that crooked smile. The small gap in the front, the one side going up higher than the other, the almost winking one eye. It always made me wonder what he was really up to! Plus it proved to be invaluable in helping us tell him and his twin brother apart. Initially Lily looked just like her mom, and more recently, well, a little like me! But in this instance she was the spitting image of her father. Mmmm…..the very image of her father. How easy it is for a child to look like their father. Most of them were just born that way. And how easy for those of us created in His image to look like our Father. We also were "born" that way. And so ask yourselves, does your face light up the room with His love? Does your smile make people wonder what you're really up to? Wait! Never mind! Forget that one! Do your eyes reveal His mercy and grace? I don't know about you but I'm going to try and be better at that "family" resemblance. And maybe when you walk into a room someone will say, "That smile looks very familiar. Oh wait…I know…she's the spitting image of her Father!"

$\mathcal{L}$AST SUNDAY I STARTED OUR MORNING WORSHIP IN AN UNUSUAL WAY. WE DID OUR pre-service song, Pastor Mike welcomed our congregation, and we started our next song. This is where the problem started because the first song was in D minor and the next was in D major. For non-musicians it's like comparing a lemon to a lime. Kind of the same but one is a little more "sour". And here's what happened. When I started the second song I forgot to change keys. Not only that, but when I realized my mistake, I tried to get back into the right key but could not for the life of me remember how that second song was supposed to go!! I just stood there fumbling around on the keyboard and trying to look like I knew what I was doing. (Always try to look like you know what you're doing!) My guitar player decided to stay with me in the wrong key. My drummer just laid down a beat and waited for me to figure it out. And my bass player just hung out on a "D" because major or minor it's all the same to him. (Bass players everywhere just said, "Hehehehe! Got that right!") I was always trained to just keep going but there are some situations where you just have to stop, back up, and take another run at it. Which was what prompted me to lift my hands from the keys and declare "WAIT! Wait, wait, wait, wait, wait!!", which effectively brought this little mishap to an end. The truth is we all face problems daily and want desperately to fix them. A better truth is, Jesus IS the answer to any "problem" we encounter. His perfection covers our imperfections. His love embraces us when we seem unlovable. And His heart surrounds our fears and releases us into His perfect peace. And that, my friends, is a beautiful sound in any key! (All the bass players just went, "Wait! Um.....what key is that?" ☺

*T*HIS WEEK'S WORSHIP TEAM STORY COMES TO YOU FROM...THE DRUMMER!! WE were doing the first song which follows the usual pattern of verse, chorus, verse, chorus, chorus, bridge, chorus, and out. We had just finished the verse and chorus and went back to the beginning. All of us except one! Our drummer, who is also a singer, thought we were doing the chorus a second time and came in all by himself singing the wrong words, on the wrong note, in the wrong place! (In his defense I forgot to give the proper signal for going back to the top. In my defense...I don't think he watches me anyway!) I started to give him "THE LOOK' (a little something I learned from my mentor to be used only when a band member has gone rogue...or goes flat!) but thought better of that idea as I've been a little on the edge lately and I could just as easily slip into weeping/sobbing as I could hysterical laughter. In this particular moment it was laughter that seized the day! It was with great effort that I managed to suppress the giggles that threatened to burst out of me. Somewhere in the second chorus I managed to pull it together. In these little incidents I try to find the lesson to be learned. And I realized that, although there are times a "good cry"is in order, there are also times when a "good laugh" is just as therapeutic. Because when giggles like that bubble up from within you, joy is released. And with joy comes hope. And with hope comes trust. And with trust comes belief. Belief that God has got you! And whatever brought tears before can now be placed in His capable hands. The beautiful truth is the joy of the Lord is our strength. And the strength of the Lord is, well, something to be joyful about! Joy...strength; strength...joy! See how that works?? A whole lot better than your drummer going rogue on you!!

Jacqualine K. Boog

*I*RECENTLY PURCHASED A NEW SILICON PARING KNIFE FROM PAMPERED CHEF. I GOT it to carry in my lunch bag to cut up my daily apple. It's a lovely neon orange with it's own little matching sheath. I thought it was odd that it came with explicit instructions as to how to use it including how to get it back in it's covering. I mean, seriously, I know how to use a paring knife. Been doing it for years. As I read through how to keep the blade away from my skin I thought, "What? Do they think I'm twelve??" Seemed ridiculous to me that one would need such detailed instructions for a knife! I have cut myself five times on said knife!! FIVE TIMES!!! (Shaking head and rolling eyes!!) I sheepishly told my son Matthew about my problem and he asked if it was time for him to come and put away all the sharp objects! I answered him with a "PFFFTTT!!" Matthew is actually a bit of a knife connoisseur and I suggested he might want to add this one to his collection. He thought that was a great idea and added, " I can display it with my others! This one is my Ninja knife. And that one over there is for skinning squirrels. But this one here........it's special. It was my mom's. She used it to slice apples until it got the best of her! It's one sharp knife! She's one tough lady!! Although sometimes she acts like a 12 year old!" Ya know…I've always wanted to be the kind of person that lives on the cutting edge. I now have FIVE wounds that prove I've taken up residence there!

A FEW WEEKS BACK I WROTE ABOUT THE WATER ON THE GREAT LAKES AND WHAT happens when it changes temperature. There is another phenomenon that always intrigues me. Sometimes a fog rolls off the big lake. It almost instantly drops the temperature by as much as 20 degrees. It decreases visibility along the shore line making it harder to see. And this huge lake that usually appears to have no end now looks like it has no beginning. It pretty much disappears from view. And the only thing that will dissipate this illusion is the sun. If the sun breaks through - the fog has to lift! When the Lord gives me these word pictures I am compelled to apply them in my life. I think about how we get overwhelmed with, oh I don't know, let's call it "stuff", and sometimes allow ourselves to become engulfed in a "fog". Our spirits become colder as the fog settles in. As we try to navigate the shores of our decisions we can't seem to see clearly. And where before we felt like there were endless possibilities, now we can't seem to find where to begin! And the ONLY thing that will dissipate this illusion is...THE SON! When you let Him in - the fog has to lift! Mother nature can be a beautiful thing but she cannot hold a candle to the Father of Creation! And remember, we can always find abundant beauty in these majestic lakes but abundant life can only be found in the Majesty that is Him!

*T*ODAY I'M GOING TO TELL YOU A STORY ABOUT TEAM WORK. IT COMES, AS MANY do, from my worship team. But that's pretty much my world! The band had rehearsed an original song for the offering. Guitar #1 had come up with an amazing lead in. (Think beginning of "My Girl".) Guitar #2 added a great electric riff. I had the keyboard set to a Hammond B-3 and was singing the lead. The drummer had a great rhythm going on, the bass was thumping it down, and we were ready to rock and roll! When the time came to play our song guitar #1 brought us in…unfortunately with a totally different lead than we had practiced. (Think "My Girl" again but this time like she is a toddler…skipping!) I wasn't even quite sure how to sing it that way. I looked at him trying to figure out where he was going with this and he just smiled at me. Guitar #2 realized the problem and simply said, "No. No. No. No." repeatedly. Guitar #1 just kept smiling! Then guitar #2 started playing the correct lead…unfortunately in the wrong key! Couldn't sing it that way either. The drummer, bass player, and I just sort of watched and waited until the other two figured it out. Once the right groove was established guitar #1 picked it up in the right key and we were off. It was clear sailing from there and we nailed it! And that's the way it should be. No one was going to let anybody fall until we were all in it together. Team work! But that's not the end of this story. Pastor Mike usually calls me back up to lead in a final song. But I had lost track of time and when he asked me to come, I was caught completely off guard. I slowly made my way to the keyboard desperately trying to think of an appropriate song when guitar #2, seeing my distress, came along side of me and simply said, "Just as I Am"! Boom!! And there it is again. Team work! One hand holding the other, and the other, and the other, and the other until we're all in it together! (Think "You've Got a Friend"!) ♫♫♫

LAST SATURDAY I HAD THE PRIVILEGE OF WATCHING OVER MY 3 YEAR OLD granddaughter, Lily. Now, usually I have a support system. This day it was just me and…THE BEAN! The day is a bit of a blur but let me share with you a few highlights! I offered her toys that my grandchildren have enjoyed for years. She was unimpressed. I gave her water in a sippy cup with a lid I have trouble getting off and on. She brought it to me 3 minutes later cup in one hand, the lid in the other and announced, "My socks are wet!" As was MY chair where she had been sitting when the incident happened! She would talk to me in a complete intelligent sentence and then start speaking in tongues! I, unfortunately, did not have the gift of interpretation. I did, however, understand one distinct word…potty! I grabbed her in my arms and ran with her up the stairs to the bathroom just in time to discover an already wet pull-up. Oops! I sat her on the potty anyway and asked if she was done. "No", she said. She sat for like 5 seconds and I asked again was she done? "Ya", she said with a smile. She had managed to deposit one…single…drop…of pee! Valiant effort Lily Bean! Obviously I gave her too much water in the afore mentioned sippy cup! (Rolling eyes!) I tried to limit my own intake of water fearing what might happen if I was in the bathroom for more than 10 seconds! Lunch was a brilliant success as I was armed with mac-n-cheese (every grandchild's favorite) and M&M's (every grandparent's bribe!). By the end of the day I had lost the ability to speak in intelligent sentences. Something I apparently picked up from my time with the Bean! You bested me sweet Lily! Final score…The Bean - 1. Grammie - 0. I declare you the winner…. for THIS day. Because there will be another and a new victor will arise!!

WHEN I WAS WALKING THE OTHER NIGHT I WAS EXPERIENCING THE SCENT OF lilacs and Lily of the Valley. Such delicate flowers with an intoxicating aroma. At the end of a hard day or a long week I would love to just sit in the midst of them for a moment, inhale deeply, and let that sweet fragrance wash over me taking the cares of this world away for a little while. The season in which they bloom is short lived but someone made a way to bottle the scent making it available to us at any time. There was a woman many years ago who actually did just the opposite. She "unbottled" her favorite scent. It was contained in an alabaster jar and was very precious to her. But she broke open that jar and poured its contents over the only One who was worthy of such an extravagance. Then she laid herself at His feet and let that intoxicating fragrance wash over her. And all those around her were suddenly in the midst of this fragrant offering. And in that short time, those gathered near were able to surrender the cares of their world. This was for only a moment but Someone made a way for us to experience His presence at any time. Some seasons in our life can seem a bit overwhelming but they are really short lived in comparison to eternity. So take the time to surrender. Pour out your fragrant offering. Inhale deeply the fragrance of your King! And let the cares of this world become His concerns, not yours. #bloomwhereyouareplanted

OUR GRANDDAUGHTER, LILY, HAS REACHED THAT 3 YEAR OLD AGE WHERE SHE thinks she can have, say or do anything. And such was the case a few nights ago when she wanted some applesauce. Being close to dinner she was told no. And she pitched the average fit of a toddler ending with trying to slap at her daddy! Matthew responded with a swat on her behind. She cried even harder and flailed her arms at him again. And his response was the same as before. She raised her hand one more time and Matthew did something Lily never expected. He reached out for her arms, pulled her in as close to him as he could and hugged this little child with all the love a father can give! Lily at first was surprised but then melted into her daddy's arms and wrapped herself around him in a hug fit for a king. And then she began to cry. Not out of anger or because she didn't get her way. But because she realized how very much her daddy loves her and in that moment she won his heart all over again. And I have to tell you that I cannot ignore the comparison I see in how much our heavenly Father loves us. He had a people who were rebellious and acting like they could have, say or do anything. He tried disciplining those He loved so very much but that didn't seem to work. And then He did what His people least expected. He stretched out His arms on a cross and then wrapped them around the hearts of His children. And our only response should be a "hug" fit for a King as we allow our hearts to be won over by Him. Lily does not yet understand the love of her Heavenly Father but I believe Matthew gave her a glimpse of what she will one day know. Well done, Matthew. Well done!

WE HAD AN UNUSUAL OCCURRENCE IN OUR SERVICE LAST SUNDAY MORNING. Not unusual for church but unusual in its timing. The worship team had just finished a nice, upbeat, hand clapping original song for the offering. It was fun and every one was having a good time with it. But as we finished there was an instant change in the atmosphere of the room. There was a hush that fell. As the team turned to leave the platform we all saw what caused the change. There was a young family who had a need and several people had gathered around them in prayer. We knew instinctively what to do. We returned to our places of ministry. Two of us began to softly play a simple melody. The third stepped to his mic and began to speak words of encouragement to the congregation, to those praying, to the people of God. And then we began to sing a tender song declaring God as our Healer. We went from rock and roll praise to passionate worship in a 60 second loop! But isn't that what we are called to be? The church being the church? Not just going into a building (although it helps to be there), not sitting in the same place each week (I do have one friend who likes to sit somewhere different every week. People treat her like she's someone new!), but being the hands and feet of God! So make yourselves available! Be in your place! (Or try out a new seat!) Be ready in season and out! Rejoice with those who rejoice and weep with those who weep! Be in your church so you can…BE THE CHURCH!!!

We visited Lily Bean the other night and she was very excited to show us her new acrobatic and dancing skills. We barely got in the door and she demonstrated her first performance. She ran at us full bore and then promptly sat down. Which took me by surprise because it was more like her run turned into a sit as she stuck her feet straight out and plopped right onto her behind! And if that's what she was going for…..nailed it!! I clapped my hands in admiration of her feat and she said, "I not done yet!" Oops! My bad! Next up was what she called a "flip" but was really more like a somersault and every time she did it she "landed" by banging into something. And again I ooh'd and aah'd over her magnificent talent and she said, "I not done yet!" And finally she would twirl herself in a circle sort of jumping through the air in the final section of the dance always landing opposite of what she meant to. I held my applause on this one until I had asked, "Are you done now?" The answer……"Ya…I done now!" (Cue applause!) And with each event she finished with a flourish; hands in the air and a brilliant smile on her face! Now I'm not writing about this story because it's adorable (although, let's face it….it is!). I'm sharing it with you because there is a wealth of wisdom to be gained and I plan on putting it into action! The next time I attempt something and end up on my behind, I'll just proclaim "I not done yet!" If I'm banging up against something preventing my perfect ending…."I not done yet!" And when I dance like no one's watching and end up facing the back wall I'm just going to throw my hands in the air, flash a brilliant smile, and proclaim, "Now I done!" (Cue applause!) There is so much truth in the words "a little child shall lead them". Just sayin'………

WE ATTENDED A JAZZ CONCERT AT OUR LOCAL LIBRARY THE OTHER NIGHT. THE gathering took place in one of their gardens so we took our camp chairs and got ready for a great night. Our pastor and his wife joined us but as we were setting up our chairs there were a few issues. To begin with Pastor Mike's chair was broken! He was a little concerned he was going to fall out of it. His wife smiled and said, "If he ends up on the ground, just throw your hands in the air and shout Hallelujah!" (This particular method, by the way, works in a multitude of situations!) She then sat down in her chair which promptly began to rock. She pulled it a little forward to more solid ground and said, "Hey....isn't there a song about that??" Um....yes, I believe there is! My husband Larry's chair was almost perfect except for the guy trying to set up a video camera in front of him. So he just positioned himself a little closer to me where he had a better view. My chair was j-u-s-t right! (Anybody else thinking Goldilocks and the Three Bears or is it just me??) We all eventually got comfortable and enjoyed a thoroughly entertaining concert which was put on by very special friends of ours. The finale, with their entire family, was indescribable!!! So, here are some points to be learned from this night. If you find yourself in a place that everything seems to be falling out from underneath you, just put your hands in the air and shout Hallelujah! If life becomes a little rocky, pull yourself up and stand on ♫The Solid Rock♫! And if you can't see clearly, change your outlook and get closer to someone who's "vision" is different than yours! There you go! A three part sermon and we never left (or fell out of) our chairs! And in the end friends, I guarantee the finale will be worth it!!! So praise God and shout Hallelujah!!

*M*Y BOYS ARE NOT "HUGGERS". OH, I GET THE OBLIGATORY HUG ON MY BIRTHDAY and on Mother's Day and if Christmas is really good for them they sometimes give out one more. But my granddaughter Lily? Now she's a hugger. It's the first thing she does when you come in the door and the last thing she does when you leave. Because that's who Lily Bean is. She is a giver of hugs! Last Wednesday The Beans had a bit of a rough day. She had a tonsillectomy in the morning, was discharged in the afternoon, and when we arrived to see her in the early evening she was all wrapped up on the couch with her favorite blankets. I sat down beside her and when she realized I was there she slid out from underneath her blankets and climbed into my lap. Like a puppy she circled three times to try and find the perfect spot which ended up being with her arms encircled around my neck and her little head nestled on my shoulder. Because sometimes you just need a Grammy hug to get you through the rest of your day. But this hug was different. Lily was not the giver of this hug, she was in need of it. Truth is we all need a hug from time to time. Life just sort of gets us down and we kind of want to wrap ourselves up and hide under our favorite blanket. But then we realize the Comforter has sat down beside us and we come out from under our blankets and climb into His lap. He will let us circle around a few times until we're comfortable and then He will hold us there until we feel like we can let go. That's just who He is! THE giver of hugs. And sometimes you just need a God hug to get you through the rest of your day!

*I*DISCOVERED THREE THINGS THE OTHER NIGHT. 1. I'M OUT OF SHAPE. 2. I SHOULD probably get more exercise. 3. I cannot run. Let me tell you how I arrived at these conclusions. We took our 3 year old granddaughter, Lily, shopping with us to give her parents a much needed break. We went to Walmart and the rule is she doesn't have to ride in the cart if she hangs on to you and stays close. She decided to "hang on to" my shirt and she was clinging to one end of it quite nicely. We had been through most of the store without any "events" and were making our way from the back to the front. I made the mistake of diverting my attention for one second and then I felt it more than saw it. When I glanced up, Lily had that look in her eye and I knew she was about to run! And so began the chase! And it looked something like this; Lily running, giggling, and stopping every 30 feet or so to make sure I saw her, me doing the "Granny" run in a feeble attempt to catch her, and an ever growing line of spectators who seemed to be cheering for each of us unable to discern at this point who was going to win! This "game" of hers continued until she was almost to the entrance of the store. At this point I became desperate and enlisted the help of a young lady just coming in. I believe my exact words were, "GRAB HER!!!" This sweet lady stopped Lily in her tracks and handed her over to me for her "sentencing"which was a swat on the behind! And then we began the walk of shame back towards where we left Papa; me at a fast walk, her hand firmly held in mine, her little feet running beside me trying to keep up! So let me just recap what I learned. 1. I'm still out of shape. 2. I no doubt need more exercise. 3. However, I can run......Granny style!!! Desperate times call for desperate measures!!

I HAVE AN OLD BAG THAT GOES WITH ME EVERYWHERE. BUT, HEY....HE'S FUN TO have around! I also have a 31 tote that is always with me whether it's to work, a short trip around town, or a longer trip out of town. In this bag are my essentials. There are almost always M&M's because......duh! There is usually a snack pack of some kind. My favorite is Teddy Grahams. I have an extra phone charger, hand cream and two essential oils. I also have an umbrella and an ear warmer because I live in Northern Michigan. The weather here changes on a dime!! And last, but not least, Angry Bird teeth flossers. (Don't ask. I have no idea!) So I'm prepared! I'm ready! I'm good to go! But what about my spiritual tote? Is it properly packed? Is the word of God settled securely in my heart so that wherever I am I can call upon it? Do I have my alabaster jar filled with "essential" oil ready to break at His feet? Do I have the garment of praise packed to be used as a covering against the spirit of heaviness? And what about prayer and praise and all of HIS favorites that He has taught me to have nearby? My 31 tote might be a little over packed. (Okay. The Angry Bird teeth flossers are probably over the top!) So I ask again….what about your spiritual tote? Are you prepared? Are you ready? Are you good to go? You have to make that decision for yourself but I will tell you this. You can never be over prepared for God because He will NEVER be under prepared for you!

*L*ARRY AND I JUST GOT BACK FROM OUR BI-ANNUAL TRIP TO "JACKIE'S WORLD". WE have stayed in the same place, in the same room for years. In fact, the manager has become a friend of ours. Our room is on the second floor with an outside set of stairs. We had arrived, unpacked, and then left to get something to eat. When we got back we headed for the stairs to our room. I'm usually in the lead but I went back to the car to get something and Larry was at the stairs ahead of me. As I turned to join him I noticed he was sort of shuffling his feet around and couldn't figure out what he was doing. Busting a move? No….not Larry. He doesn't dance. Then, with wide eyed realization, I saw what was causing his fancy moves! He was trying to move a SNAKE that had come out from underneath the stairwell! By my estimation it was at least 6 feet long. He said it was at most 18 inches. He clearly needs a vision check! He continued to maneuver the snake out of my way and I hesitantly moved towards him repeatedly asking if snakes can climb stairs! He assured me that they would not. They prefer elevators! Not funny! Not helpful! Once in our room I messaged my friend the manager, told him the situation and calmly declared I would not be leaving my room until the snake was found! He sent someone right away to search for the culprit and messaged me a few minutes later with the good news that the snake had been found and thrown out back somewhere! Seriously……did they disable its GPS system?? For the next few days we had a process of coming and going. Larry would go ahead, scout for any snakes, and then yell back at me, "Clear!" and we would move on. I don't usually have rules in Jackie's World but there's one in place now! Snakes are NEVER allowed! Ever! Under no circumstances! Nope! Notta!!!!!

ADVENTURE NUMBER TWO IN JACKIE'S WORLD. ON OUR LAST NIGHT THERE Larry and I went to a couple of our favorite photo op places for a beautiful sunset. When we got back to our room I noticed the long necklace I had been wearing was missing. Because of a few selfies we had taken we were able to pinpoint exactly where I lost it; somewhere on the edge of the shore at McGulpin Point. I then remembered I had my camera hanging around my neck while we were walking around. I took it off to take a picture and when I did I must have removed my necklace as well. We thought about going out to look for it but it was already dark. I was concerned that a huge black bear had found it and was roaming around the forest with my necklace dangling from its neck. I was more concerned that a huge black bear would find ME as I was looking for my lost necklace! No...we would wait until morning. So as I went to sleep that night I prayed about it. (There is no request too small for God. If it concerns you it concerns Him.) The next morning we went straight to McGulpin Point. I began to search in the area where I was pretty sure I had been standing. But I get easily distracted and when I look for something it goes kind of like this......rocks, rocks, pretty rocks, lake shore, beautiful waves, Mighty Mac.........wait! What am I looking for??? When Larry looks for something he is more like......rocks, rocks, rocks, rocks, NECKLACE!! There it was! I had become distracted and never saw it on the path. So here's the lesson learned. Sometimes when we pray about something it requires an action on our part. If we are easily distracted by things around us we may walk right past what God needs us to do. So my advice is to pray, stay focused on the right path, and let God do what He does best......find the lost! Otherwise, it's quite possible your lost treasure may become "bling" on some forest creature!!

ONE MORE STORY FROM JACKIE'S WORLD. THE DAY BEFORE WE LEFT WE DECIDED to have lunch at Kentucky Fried Chicken in Mackinaw. (Cause who doesn't love a bucket of the Colonel's best!) As we were eating I noticed a family that came in. They purchased their meal and took it to go. When we left we walked passed them gathered around a bench getting ready to eat with their toddler perched on her daddy's shoulders and three teens sitting on the bench. And then I watched as they bowed their heads and prayed! I waited until they were through and told them what a wonderful thing it was to see a family praying together. We chatted a little and went our own way. And I thought someone is always watching what you do. I encountered this family again when I went to my favorite fudge shop. The toddler was standing outside the shop big brown eyes gazing at the chocolaty goodness inside. Her mom was calling her to come but she just stood there giving her parents "the look". (Those of you with toddlers know what I'm talking about!) Her daddy asked if she was being disobedient because she didn't move except to add a pout to her batting eyes. I didn't see what happened after that because I unashamedly entered the store and got my slice of chocolaty goodness! But, again, I thought someone is always watching what you do. And now the end of my story. My husband has what he thinks is a very funny response to a simple question. "Larry, will you say grace?" His answer is ALWAYS the same. "Grace!" It's tradition. We were at McDonalds one night with Matthew, Jennifer and Lily. We sat down with our meal and just as I'm getting ready to ask Larry to say grace, Matthew says, "Wait. I got this." He turns to Lily and asks, "Lily, will you say grace?" And she responded just as her Papa does…with a smile and "grace"! Nailed it, Lily Bean! But let me remind you one more time…someone is always watching what you do!

*L*AST WEEKEND WE HAD A SMALL PROBLEM. WE LOST OUR PHONE. OKAY…I LOST our phone. Not a cell, an actual cordless phone; 1 of a 3 part set because I actually believe that we still need a "home" phone! And before I go any further let me just pause and say it had been a tiring, busy week and Saturday and Sunday proved to be a bit challenging as well! I usually put the phone on the footstool by the glider upstairs on the weekends for easy access. I noticed it was missing Saturday afternoon. We tried using the locator button found on each base. We called home from a cell phone. I checked the basement, the front porch, every bedroom, and even the freezer. Because….you know. I finally gave up and decided that it had somehow broken and wasn't responding or had been removed from our house. When the weekend was finally coming to a close I took a nice hot bath, tried to relax and think. I decided to retrace my steps from the previous day. Nothing unusual in the morning but when I got to the afternoon I remembered something. I had purchased some new hair brushes and I took them upstairs to replace the old ones which I put on the footstool by the glider to be thrown away along with some papers and other things I needed to take down stairs and….oh oh…… I opened the bathroom door and yelled down to Larry. "Try that locator thing again and this time go listen in the garbage!" He said, "Seriously?! And I said, "YES! Don't ask!" A few minutes later he shouted up to me that the lost had been found. He asked how I knew to look there. I simply replied, "I don't want to talk about it!" Apparently I threw the phone away with the old hair brushes! Most of my friends truly enjoyed this moment of blondness but my son Matthew had the best response. He said, and I quote, "I am going to come by and randomly take things from the house. And then you'll be like….has anybody seen the remote? I just used the toaster this morning! Okay……where is my microwave!!" ☺

$\mathcal{E}$VERY ROOM IN MY HOUSE HAS A "GIFT" THAT WAS GIVEN TO ME BY ONE OF MY KIDS or grandkids. Each one a treasure that reminds me of those I love. From my children: there is a lamp that Michael made when he was in shop class a long time ago. Matthew gave me a beautiful frame with a picture of us hugging after his wedding, smile on his face, tears in my eyes, and it sits on the buffet. Mark's gift is a multi-colored ball that he hides every time he visits from Arizona. It's in the….ah….well…a room somewhere! From my grandchildren: I have a little robot guy made of plastic connectors that Elliott made when he was younger and it hangs on the wall. Brynn colored pictures of princesses and taped them to the baseboard in the dining room. Ariel has gathered pebbles and seashells from the beach and acorns from the yard and they have a special place in a stoneware dish in the kitchen. And Lily Bean's offering is a snow globe with a picture of the two of us floating inside. Did you know our Father's house is much the same? It says so in His word. All the treasures we have given are stored with Him. The gift of our worship becomes a fragrant offering that fills the courtrooms of Heaven. The gift of our love freely given resides in His heart. Even the tears we shed have been captured by Him because they are special in His eyes. Each one a treasure that reminds Him of those He loves! Given by you…. safe with Him. So let us be reminded of the original gift God gave when He wrapped His love in an infant and gave Him to each of us. A treasure beyond measure to remind us of those He loves!

*L*ARRY WAS HELPING ME FINISH DECORATING THE TREE (JUST DAYS BEFORE Christmas) and I was grumbling and complaining about being tired and busy and not having enough time to get things done. And I said, "I don't know why we even do this. We're the only ones here!" And without missing a beat, he tossed the ribbon to me that we were wrapping around the tree and said, "Then we do it just for you and me!" Well, okay! So we finished the tree and I was going to call it good when I remembered one more "decoration" that needed to come out of its box in the attic...our Nativity set which should be on the priority list of decorating! Because what are the ornaments without the manger filled with hay? What is the star on top of the tree without the angels singing their glory hallelujahs? And what are the presents under the tree without the presence of the Christ child? They are meaningless without the road to Bethlehem. So I'll put up my Nativity set even if it's not until Christmas Eve (which looks like my best shot at this point) and maybe I'll leave it out longer than usual as a reminder that we should try not to let ourselves get bogged down by the busyness of the season. That we shouldn't be discouraged by the things we did or didn't do. And that we should remember the joy, peace and love of the wonder of Christmas! Because you know what? He did it all....just for you and me!!

Jacqualine K. Boog

*A*BOUT A MONTH AGO I HAD A COUPLE OF GIGS. NO REALLY!! I GOT TO USE MY gig bag and everything! I even had a "roadie"! (Okay…it was my husband…whatever!) Our friend Tom asked my husband and I to join him for a fundraiser for the local food pantries and a Christmas tea for a lovely group of ladies. Both events went very well and we had a wonderful time. But there was a small glitch at the ladies tea. We were doing a nice Christmas song in three part harmony with Tom leading on guitar and me on piano. After the first verse Tom looked at me and said, "STOP." And I thought, "Stop what? Singing? Playing? Breathing?" I opted for the first two since breathing was a necessity! So I lifted my hands from the keys, stepped back from my mic and waited. Tom continued to play and sing. I looked at him to see if I could figure out what he was doing and he just smiled. (Tom smiles a lot.) As he started the next verse I looked at him again with raised eyebrows and my hands back on the keys. He smiled and nodded and I joined back in. (Again with the smiling!) So why did he tell me to stop? Apparently he didn't! What he had actually said was TOP which in music lingo means go back to the beginning. Oops…my bad! And let me point out here that piano players can give directions with one hand while playing with the other. Not so much with guitar players hence the misunderstanding. So, do I have a moral to this story? Not really. Did it matter that I stopped singing when I did? Nope…Tom kept singing. Did it matter that I stopped playing? Nope…Tom kept playing. Did it matter that I misunderstood his directions? Nope….Tom just kept on smiling. Seriously, the guy is always smiling! He just never….wait for it…STOPS!!! And honestly what can "TOP" that!! Ha!!

I HAD A CONVERSATION THE OTHER NIGHT WITH MY 3 YEAR OLD GRANDDAUGHTER. It started with her daddy asking her if she knew what his name was. She said, "Daddy!" (What else would it be?) And then he asked her what my name was. Her response…..Gramma! (Of course!) So then I told her what my real name is. Jacqualine Kay Boog. She laughed hysterically at that obviously unable to understand how I was saddled with such a difficult name! (Plus I'm pretty sure she couldn't say it!) And so she declared, "No, you're Gramma!" I then asked what her name was to which she replied, "Lily." And I followed that with, "What's the rest of your name?" Without missing a beat she replied, "Lily Bean!" Now, in her defense, that is a nickname that was given to her before she was even born. She has always been Lily Bean to us or sometimes The Bean or as Auntie Murp (now there's a nickname…right Murp??) and Uncle Mark call her…..simply "Beans". The truth is we all have more than one name. Besides Gramma, I'm also Jackson, a name given to me by my musical buddies. And some friends simply call me Jack. These nicknames are all given in love. But here's something interesting. Lily and I have a name that we share. It was given to us by our Father in Heaven before we were even born. He calls us…. Chosen…Beloved…Child….and there is no doubt these names are given in love! And even though Lily Bean doesn't understand that yet, I believe that one day, just as the Lord called Samuel, He will call Lily's name and she will respond, "Here I am Lord…….it's me…..The Beans!!!" And He will say, "I know that name! And I love you so very much my Lily Bean!"

*P*ASTOR MIKE HAS BEEN PREACHING ON THE LORD'S PRAYER TAKING IT APART VERSE by verse. Last week he spoke on being forgiven and forgiving others. He quoted the line that says, "Forgive those who sin against you." What I heard him say was, "Forgive those who sit next to you." Mmm. Isn't that kind of taking the "you're sitting in my seat" thing a little too far? And sometimes I don't know the person sitting next to me all that well. What am I supposed to forgive him for?? Or, quite often there's no one sitting next to me at all. What am I supposed to do with that? Well, obviously I misunderstood what was said but this did allow some food for thought. Because maybe we take offense to something that really is kind of trivial. (Sitting in my chair.) Or maybe we don't really know the person we are holding something against and they have been through something we are not even aware of. Maybe words or actions were not entirely directed at us. And lastly, maybe there's nothing there at all to be upset about. There is no sin against us. (No one sitting next to us.) We've just allowed ourselves to carry a grudge over nothing (or no one). We all know that unforgiveness is only hurting us and although it's not always easy to do, let's try to let some things go. Let's forgive and be forgiven. Let's open our hearts and our minds and let God do the cleansing He needs to do. But for Heaven's sake….. please DO NOT sit in my chair! Just sayin……..#sameseateverySunday #easy accesstomykeyboard#ocd

A FEW WEEKS BACK WE HAD OUR ANNUAL OFFICE APPRECIATION PARTY. WE WERE served a lovely dinner followed by a little competitive bowling!! I had the option of participating or not and given the fact that MANY years ago I was a fairly good league bowler and in more recent years a champ at WII bowling I decided why not?? As we got ready to begin someone stood up and said, "Anybody want to use the gutter bumpers?" I laughed along with everybody else and said, "Yes, me!" Which started another round of laughter. They were apparently not being serious! I was!! Then began the team selections. Visions of recess ran through my head as I remembered usually being the last one chosen. But, much to my surprise, I was put on the "pro" team. The BEST bowlers! Yes!! Wait! The pros?? NO! Now I'm really going to look bad! I went to the counter to get my size 8 ½'s and began my search for a lightweight ball. The rest of my team came prepared with their own equipment. You know, shoes with special grip soles, wrist supports, and custom bowling balls! As I made my first approach I could barely breathe! I grabbed my ball, assumed the bowler stance, and tried to look like I knew what I was doing. I happened to remember I used to have a pretty mean left curve. So I aimed for the right. My ball did in fact curve….right….into the left gutter!! As did the next three balls after that! My third time up I hesitated a moment like I was concentrating. I was really praying, "Please Lord, let me hit something!" I had hoped I might at least end with a score of 100. My final total was 53! (I just rolled my eyes so hard you could literally hear it!) But there was a silver lining. I won a prize for the lowest individual score! And it gets better! I also won a prize for being on the highest scoring team! Ha!! I would love to impart some sage advice from this enlightening experience but I don't think I can "spare" any!! Bahahahahaa!!

S O I FINALLY LET LARRY GET A DRONE. HE'S BEEN WANTING ONE FOR SOME TIME now and we found one ½ off, I had a coupon, and well, it was just an offer we couldn't refuse! Might not have been exactly what he wanted but it was only $10.00, it fits in the palm of his hand, and after a good charge you've got 8-10 minutes of pure entertainment! A few weeks ago our grandson Elliott was at our house. He tried his skills at flying this little drone. He maneuvered it very well but landings seemed to be a bit of a challenge. He set it down once under the couch (not sure how he managed that), then pretty close to the top of my head, and finally nailed it with a 3 point landing right in the middle of a vase of dried lavender. (And let me just interject here that our son Michael, Elliott's dad, was also given a gift of a small drone a few years ago. He landed it on top of a candle…that was lit…and it continued to fly…with it's propellers on fire! Apparently it's a family thing!) Now this bouquet of lavender has been there for quite some time and had long since lost its scent. But when the drone landed it broke a few twigs and several dried flowers fell off. I went to clean them up and realized the entire room was beginning to fill with the fragrance of that lavender. When it broke what was already within it was released! And here it comes. (The application not the drone)! All of us go through dry spells, feeling like we are in the desert. But if we are willing to bend a little, if we can get rid of (or drop off) a few old, dried up things, then maybe, in that brokenness, what was already within us will be released! And your entire life will fill with a sweet fragrance! So, I'm probably not the first one to use or discover this illustration, however I'm pretty sure I'm the first that was reminded of this lesson by a mini drone!!

WEDNESDAY NIGHT AT PRAYER MEETING PASTOR MIKE ASKED US WHAT OUR understanding of God's love is and what that meant to us. We had some very good discussion about this but as we sat there sharing our experiences it occurred to me that not everybody fully understands how great God's love is. Maybe some have not had an earthly father who displayed love like our Heavenly Father. There are those who don't know what unconditional love is. Or possibly others have been let down by family or friends with every betrayal leaving a broken piece and every misspoken word leaving a wound until there is so much hurt they begin to shut down parts of themselves because they don't want to feel that way again. But if we can't comprehend God's love how can we receive it? And if we can't receive it how can we give it? Only by allowing that love to seep into our hearts are we able to give it away, unconditionally. God's love is pure. It's the kind of love that would make Him leave Heaven just to come after you. That would embrace you just as you are because He knows who you will be. That carried the cross to Calvary, every betrayal breaking a piece of Him, every word spoken against him leaving a wound, and even though He could have "shut down" all the pain he was enduring He did not because you were on His heart! His own life was being given for you! This is not my usual kind of story. There are no "Jackie-isms" as my husband calls them. It's just my heart to yours, one imperfect person to another, hoping we can all learn to receive the Perfect Love of God. So remember as we celebrate this Easter week, "greater love has no one than this". Believe it my friends! Receive it!! And then give it away!!

A FEW MONTHS AGO WHEN THERE WAS STILL SNOW ON THE GROUND LARRY AND I took Lily Bean to Walmart with us. She was perfect, holding my hand most of the way through the store and then in the parking lot on our way to the car. As a matter of fact, she held on so well that she slipped on some dirty snow and went down and back up, her hand still in mine, and I didn't even know it! That's the best Gramma in the world award right there! (Insert rolling eyes!) When I realized she had slipped I checked her over and asked if she was okay. She said yes but was very worried about her brand new unicorn leggings. There was a very noticeable dirty stain right on her knee and she was more concerned with that than any injury. I assured her that we could get the stain out and her beautiful leggings would be good as new. And I might add here that this apparently made quite an impression on her because the next time we took her to Walmart she reminded me of the incident and wanted to make sure I would NOT let her fall in the mud again! Nope! Won't happen! Not on my watch!! But the whole thing reminded me of how I once was. I was stained from falling down too many times and I felt like I would never be clean again. But Jesus picked me up out of the miry clay. He set my feet on solid ground. He brushed away all the dirt and stains and said, "It's okay child. I can remove the stains and make you brand new!" And just like Lily needed to know I would not let her fall again, I sometimes have to remind myself that as long as I keep my hand in His, I am safe with Him. And if at some time I should happen to slip and fall again, He will pick me up, brush me off and say, "Don't worry! I've got you! Let me help you remove that stain." So, all that being said......anybody know where I can get a pair of unicorn leggings? Cause I haven't seen the Beans wear hers since I dropped her in the dirt!! (Again with the rolling eyes!!)

A FEW SUNDAYS AGO MY SON MARK WAS TRYING TO CALL ME. HE DIDN'T GET hold of me until in the afternoon. This is kind of how our conversation went:

Mark: Mom! Where have you been??? I had a worship leading crisis!!!

Me: I was playing for a wedding! What happened??

Mark: Well, I had just finished the first song and was going into the next one and I couldn't find my note! I tried but I totally missed it! Wasn't even close! It sounded terrible!

Me: (Stifling laughter.) It happens to the best of us Mark. It's okay.

Mark: That's not the worst of it. I went back for the second round of the song and did the same thing........again!!!

Me: Bahahahaha! (No longer able to stifle laughter!) That's the best thing you could have done! It's a well known fact that if you make a mistake in a song you do the same thing the second time around and people will think you meant to do it that way! Works for me every time!

Mark: I'm pretty sure the Lord released me from my calling as a worship leader right then and there! Not only that but I thought I heard a trumpet. Probably God trying to drown out the sound I was making!!

Me: Or maybe He was calling for Gabriel, "Get over here quick! I've got another worship leader gone rogue!!!" But remember this because it's the truth. God didn't hear any off key notes. Because He is not looking for perfection. He is looking for heart intention. And I know your heart was seeking to honor Him. Unfortunately your vocal chords were seeking something else.....the right note perhaps?? ☺ And, Mark, God would never drown out your song because to Him it was a joyful sound! I mean, seriously, I didn't even hear it and look how much "joy" it has given me!!

OUR FOUR YEAR OLD GRANDDAUGHTER'S NAME IS LILY. BUT BEFORE SHE WAS EVEN born we nicknamed her Lily Bean or simply "The Beans". The following story will explain why. She stayed overnight with us last Friday. We picked her up at her house. She was packed and ready to go. And just as we were ready to leave she ran to her mama, gave her a great big "Lily" hug, and said, "I'm sorry!" Her mama asked, "What are you sorry about?" And Lily said, "I have to leave you now. But I'll come back!" How sweet is that! This little one wanted to make sure her mama would be okay while she was gone! That my friends is……our Lily! ♥ The next day Papa and I took her to Dairy Grille, our local ice cream shop, and got her a favorite treat…. soft serve chocolate ice cream in a cup, not a cone. I handed it to her and she squealed with delight and then said, "Gramma, this looks like a piece of poop!" (I have to be honest, swirled in the cup the way it was, she was kind of right. It looked like one of those emojis.) This startling revelation obviously did not concern her because she was truly enjoying her treat. But after a couple of spoonfuls she started to giggle and declared, "I look like I'm eating a piece of poop!" And that my friends is…..The Beans! Now some have said that Lily is a lot like her Mama. And that's true. But…Beans??? She's just like her Gramma!! ☺

WERE YOU ALL AWARE THAT WE HAVE LONGER DAYS HERE IN NORTHERN Michigan than some of the south/east states? That at 8:00 or so in North Carolina it is already dark while it is still daylight until almost 9:00 here?? We are in the same time zone. We all do the daylight savings time change. What's the deal?? Apparently it has to do with the rotation of the earth, the fact that we are so far north, and something about the equator. Really? I found out this epic piece of information on a Sunday just before the worship team's pre-service prayer time. Pastor Mike was trying to explain the why's and how's of this but it made absolutely no sense in my mind! And yet, it was hard NOT to think about it. A little bit later we started our normal morning service. The first worship song was about how the Lord rescued us and saved us. When the song ended Pastor Mike reminded us while it was true we have been rescued and saved God is also in the present and encouraged us to sing the song again in the present tense. I kind of stared at him and actually said out loud, "You're blowing my mind this morning Mike! You're blowing my mind!" So now I'm really put to the test as I'm trying to play the song, change the words as I go to reflect present tense (rescues/saves) and still remain Spirit led!!! As our worship time was over I sat down and Mike began his message. I was following pretty well until he came to.......the pump story! From the way I understood it, in order to get water OUT of a well, you have to pour water IN to the well! Oh! Come! On! At this point I gave up and started doodling in my notebook! So if anyone else has some startling new facts you want to share with me, good luck with that! #informationoverload#isitnightor-day#spirituallycorrectgrammar#waterinwaterout

A FEW SUNDAYS AGO I HAD A BIT OF A WORSHIP SITUATION. WE WERE DOING A song in 6/8 time which has a waltz feel. I was going into the chorus and got lost. And the thing is with 6/8 timing if you miss the downbeat you will be forever stuck in a runaway loop!! (It's kind of like trying to jump onto a moving merry-go-round. If you miss you'll end up on your behind!) Just when I thought we were never going to get out of what we now refer to as the never ending song, I heard what I can only describe as a still, small voice. It was my guitar player very softly singing the words I needed to get back into the song. I jumped in and just like that I was exactly where I was supposed to be! God bless guitar players everywhere! I thought I had pulled it off without too many people noticing but alas....no. Apparently my predicament was exactly what Pastor Mike needed to bring the point home in his message (you're welcome!) and referred to it repeatedly in the last 15 minutes of his sermon! (Thank you!) But you know what? I got just what I needed as well! A little help from my friends! Plus an added personal application. Because I sometimes feel like there's so much going on in my life that I get lost and can't figure out how to get back onto the merry-go-round of life without falling on my behind! But if I quiet myself and listen I can hear that still, small voice whispering the very words I need. "Come to Me! I'll show you the way!" And if I follow Him, just like that I'll land exactly where I'm supposed to be! And who knows. Maybe as you learn how to get back on that merry-go-round it will be the very thing someone else needs to help them find where they need to be and keep them from landing on their behind! #igetbywithalittlehelpfrommyfriends#roundan-droundwego#nooneleftontheirbehind

LARRY AND I WERE HELPING WITH MOVING SOME THINGS AROUND IN OUR CHURCH sanctuary. One of them was a huge wooden cross which stands in the corner of the front platform and needed to go to the other side of the room. I was going to offer to carry it but…..pftttt…like that was going to happen! What I did do was help remove some of the decorations that were around the base of the cross. To my surprise what was supporting our cross was a very large Christmas tree stand. What? The cross was in a Christmas tree stand?? I could not stop thinking about this word picture because to me it was Christmas and Easter all rolled up in one! I tiny "piece" of a traditional Christmas was holding up the cross! I mean, think about it. What does a Christmas tree stand do? It gives the tree support. It keeps it from swaying to the left or to the right. It provides water to keep its branches fresh, soft, and never dried up. And then I thought….what does the cross do? It gives us support. It keeps us from swaying to the left or the right. It keeps our hearts watered with the Word so that it remains fresh, soft and never dried up. So by my calculations…….Christmas leads us to the cross. The cross leads us to Jesus. Jesus comes into our hearts. And our hearts are turned to the King…born on CHRISTMAS day! Full circle, my friends, full circle!! So, maybe that was a lot of words that were kind of jumbled together but the whole cross in the Christmas tree stand really brought it home for me. And keep in mind…..this is MY thought process we are talking about and seriously, if I don't keep my thoughts in perfect order I'm like……. Christmas…..cross…..Easter…..bunnies…..PEEPS!……squirrel!!!!!!!

*I*HAVE A BEAUTIFUL WEDDING RING. IT WAS ACTUALLY CREATED JUST FOR ME. I cherish it. It means I belong to my husband. A while back I decided to make meatloaf for dinner and took my ring off before preparing it because no one wants ground beef stuck in their diamonds! I put it in my pocket. When the meatloaf was in the oven I went to the living room and sat down in my chair to check my phone. From there I went to the bathroom. As I was washing my hands I realized I hadn't put my ring back on and reached in my pocket to get it. It wasn't there! And so I began my search! I briefly wondered if it had somehow gotten in the meatloaf and was now baking its way to perfection! I couldn't see how that would have happened but decided if I didn't find it no one was eating that meatloaf! Next I went through the garbage because, well, several months ago I found our phone in there! (Don't ask!) It wasn't in there. My next stop was the chair in the living room. I went through the cushions, moved pillows, got down on my hands and knees and searched the floor. Again, nothing! And finally I went back to the bathroom. Maybe it fell out of my pocket in there. Sometimes your search becomes desperate and in that desperation I actually checked the toilet and will confess to a silent, yet fervent prayer of, "Please dear God! Don't let it be in there!!" It was not!! Thank you Jesus! My last attempt was to retrace every step I had taken and keep my eyes on the floor. And there in my bedroom, sparkling on the carpet, was my ring. It was then I remembered I had taken a kleenex out of that same pocket and my ring obviously came out with it. And folks, my search for my ring is nothing compared to the Lord's search for His loved ones. He is relentless in His pursuit, desperate in His search! He will go through the garbage, move what needs to be moved, look in every possible place until He finds the lost. Because we were created for Him. He cherishes us. And we belong to Him. My ring was lost and I searched until I found it. I was lost and He searched until He found me! #iwaslostbutnowiamfound#desperatetimescallfordesperatemeasures #thankyouGoditwasnotinthetoity

*L*ARRY AND I TOOK A NICE EVENING STROLL THE OTHER NIGHT. WE WERE WALKING and talking when out of nowhere a bug hit me smack on the lips. Surprisingly my mouth was actually closed at that particular moment! I brushed it away (several times to be sure it was gone) and we continued our walk. But something didn't feel right and I abruptly stopped walking and said, "Hold on! Wait a minute!". I then proceeded to lift my shirt just a tad and reached up under it to adjust my....um...undergarment and then, and my apologies as there is no other way to describe this, began to....well.....jiggle! Larry looked at me and said, "What. Are. You. Doing???" I started to explain to him that I was pretty sure that bug had gone down my shirt when he suddenly stamped his foot in front of me! At this point we kind of looked like we were trying to bust a move on the dance floor! Unlikely, although if I'd had a paddle I would have given us a solid 7! Then he said, "I got it!" I asked, "The bug? Are you sure it was my bug? Did you see it come out of my shirt??" He said yes on all accounts but not without a nice eye roll! Satisfied that the problem was solved we began walking again although I will admit to a few additional "jiggles" because I just couldn't "shake" the feeling that it was still in there! So what else can I say about this?? Nothing except that's what it's like........living in Jackie's World!! #ithinksomebodywroteabookbythattitle #neveradullmoment#soyouthinkyoucandance

Last weekend I took my granddaughters, Brynn and Lily, down to the library to see the last of the monarch butterflies still hanging around. There were only a couple but one flew right over Lily's head. She froze, eyes like saucers, hands covering her mouth, standing completely still in awe of this beautiful creature that had nearly kissed her face! The look on her little face was indescribable! Our next stop was the playground where Lily wanted to try out the swing. So Brynn and I helped her into it and offered to give her a push. Lily assured us she knew how to do it and then just sat there pretty much doing nothing. So I asked again if I could give her a little push. And also if she knew how to pump her legs. She said yes and yes and I gave her the slightest push and said, "Pump your legs Lily!" She then proceeded to do the best running man impression I've ever seen! Her little legs started running furiously catching nothing but air and her swing barely moved an inch. But here's the thing. Lily was not upset by this at all. And again, the look on her face was indescribable. She was smiling from ear to ear! It didn't matter that she was getting absolutely nowhere. She was giving it her all enjoying every minute of her "run"! Wow! I have learned a lot through the eyes of a child and I'm going to put this one to work right away. Because, seriously, how often do we feel like we are furiously running and getting absolutely no where? So I'm going to watch for butterflies and be in awe of the beauty that surrounds me. I will do the best I can at whatever I'm doing. I will be less concerned with how far I'm getting and more concerned with enjoying the "run" to get there! And once in awhile I'm going to find myself a swing and just sit there doing pretty much nothing! Basically I'm going to be more like a child! Although it's quite possible that ship may have already sailed!

THE FRONT OF OUR CHURCH HAS A HUGE BELL TOWER WITH A BEAUTIFUL LIGHTED cross on the front that can be seen from the highway. One evening I called Pastor Mike to talk to him about the upcoming Sunday service. He answered his phone and said, "You'll never guess what I'm doing!" "What?", I asked. He then proceeded to tell me he was sitting in his lawn chair outside the church watching the bell tower to see if he could figure out where bats were getting in and out of the church. He said, "Yup, I'm staring at the cross watching for bats!" I said, "E-e-w-w-w!" But I also warned him that this incident might end up in my musings on Facebook because honestly that right there will preach! Plus it's a perfect example of a pastor going above and beyond to watch over his flock! The more I thought about it the more I realized how we can apply this little tidbit to our lives. How often do we allow thoughts to fly in and out of our minds causing us concern, worry, and fear? (And believe me when I say if one of those bats ever fly through the sanctuary during a service you will most definitely see me fly under the keyboard!!) So how do we get rid of them? By finding the source of their coming and going and seal off that door freeing your mind to think upon those things that are true, noble, just, pure, lovely, and of a good report! Meditate on these things. And just like Pastor Mike, keep your eyes on the cross. An age old song says, "Turn your eyes upon Jesus and the things of earth will grow strangely dim in the light of His glory and grace." Look into His light! Bell towers will always be a hiding place for bats. The cross will always be a hiding place for God's people!

Jacqualine K. Boog

O UR HOME IS AT LEAST 100 YEARS OLD AND WITH THAT COME A FEW QUIRKS. For instance, there is little to no closet space and we've had to become creative in some areas. In our bedroom there is no closet at all but we improvised by hanging racks and shelves in a 6 ft by 4 ft space in the corner of the room. I think it must have been an entrance way of some sort years ago because it has a door that opens into the dining room. I suppose technically it could be considered a "walk in" closet so...ha!! Which leads me to my story. I used that particular door the other night because it actually is a quicker way into the bedroom from that end of the house. The door stuck as I opened it and it was then that I remembered I had left my pink Minnetonka moccasins on the floor just inside the "closet". And now one of them was stuck under the door. I tried everything to move it and couldn't get it loose. I pulled, I pushed, I tried to smoosh it under but it would not come out. And I didn't want it to rip or tear because, duh.....it's a pink, Minnetonka moccasin! I finally gave up and yelled for help. "Larry, will you come to the closet door and help me??" He came and found me sitting behind the half open door on the floor looking at my moccasin. I explained the situation to him and began to tug and pull in demonstration and he said, "Stop! Stop, stop, stop! Why don't you just slide it down to the end of the door?" I said, "What??" and then kind of grinned and said, " Oh..........!" My moccasin slid out like I had buttered it! Not a scratch on it. Larry took his seat back in the living room but not before he added, "What would you do without me??" I considered that for a moment and then said, "I don't know! But I would probably be walking around wearing only one pink, Minnetonka moccasin!!"
#hellomynameisjackieandiamablonde#ontheupsidewedohavemorefun
#onlybecausewefindourselvessoamusing

ON OUR RECENT TRIP TO JACKIE'S WORLD I BOUGHT A PIECE OF JEWELRY. OKAY I bought two pieces of jewelry. And a sweatshirt, um…hand cream, a candle, and a photograph from our favorite photographer. Oh…..and fudge because…duh! (These are perks of reigning as queen in Jackie's World. I pretty much get whatever I want!) But it's the first piece of jewelry that my story is about. It's a ring set with a small, uncut Canadian diamond. I knew when I laid my eyes on it I wanted it. (See above.) Not because of it's outward appearance but because of what it represents. It's a diamond in the rough. Even the band that holds it is not perfect. It has uneven edges and an unpolished look. But in the hands of a master jeweler it could be chiseled and refined to become a brilliant, sparkling princess cut diamond. Now I'm talking mostly to the ladies here but don't we all feel this way sometimes? Not quite perfect? Marred around the edges? Not as brilliant as we'd like to be? A diamond in the rough. I'm not always the best wife, mom, grandma, or even friend that I could be. I fail miserably on occasion. And yet in the Master's Hand I am being chiseled, refined and made into the beautiful "Princess" cut He sees in me. To look at my ring it is not very impressive. But when you look at it through the eyes of one who sees its potential, it shines. And that's the way your Father looks at you. He doesn't look at the outward appearance. He looks deeper at what's inside. He sees your potential and you shine! Now, on a side note…my ring was marked down to half off. Plus there was a special sale going on and it was reduced by another 50%! (Because that's the way we roll in Jackie's World!) It's price was decreased but not its value. And your value is ever increasing in the eyes of your Father. You are priceless…..a diamond in the rough!

SUNDAY BEFORE LAST THE WORSHIP TEAM WAS DOING OUR PRE-SERVICE PRAYER time. Pastor Mike ended by saying, "Lord we give You all our attention." What I heard him say was, "Lord we give You all our tension." Now I'm not sure if I've got some hearing issues or if my mind was wandering (both are completely possible) but it made me stop and think. The Lord clearly tells us NOT to worry and to cast ALL our cares on Him. And yet we struggle day in and day out with issues that take our attention away from Him and place them right back on whatever is causing the tension. I'll be honest with you and say there are many days that I wake up in the morning and it's an effort to get out of bed. (My husband says I'm the queen of worry but I'm also the queen of Jackie's World so…ha!) I don't want to face the "tension/stress" in my life and so I mumble a quick prayer and ask God to just let me get one foot in front of the other and make it through the day. But He does so much more than that. He manages to fill the day I was dreading with joy, peace and even laughter. All because I was willing to give Him my attention. So I don't think it was a hearing issue that morning. I'm guessing my mind was wandering and I forgot where my attention should be. And maybe what I thought I heard Mike say was exactly what I was supposed to hear. Because if you are willing to give Him all your attention He is more than willing to take all your tension. It's as easy (and as hard) as that. So if you'll excuse me I guess I better start practicing what I preach 'cause I'm starting to feel a little tense!! And also maybe I'll schedule a hearing test because, well, you know……just in case!

*A*T THIS TIME OF YEAR IT IS SO EASY TO BECOME EXTRAVAGANT IN OUR GIVING especially when it comes to our children. We tend to not even think about the cost. Because our joy comes in the smile on their faces when they see what we have given them. And this year is no exception for me as I have already over-done with some shopping. I am very excited about some of my gifts and I feel pretty comfortable sharing with you what I got for my boys because, although my lovely daughters-in-law read every word I write, my three sons stop after about four lines! But before I go any further let us never forget, as they say, the reason for this season. A gift given to all of us so very long ago. A Father who so wanted to see joy in the lives of His children gave a gift of such value that Heaven and earth rejoiced in it's coming. God sent His only son for us. A gift like no other, it was extravagant beyond belief. He never considered the cost. And no other gift could possibly give us more joy than this One did. A baby born in lowly means that would one day wear a crown as the King of Kings. That is why we give extravagantly and share lovingly at this time of year. So to finish the rest of my story I will now let you know what I did for the boys. They told me what they wanted but they are going to be so excited when they see their gift. I truly went above and beyond and got each of them…….. wait!……did you really think I would say it?? But I'm guessing, my sweet sons, that I made you read my whole story!!! Falalalalalalalala!!! ♫♫♫

WE HAD OUR FAMILY GATHERING AFTER CHRISTMAS WHILE OUR SON MARK WAS here. But it was his twin brother Matthew that brought down the house with his gift giving. Matthew arrived at the house with a garbage bag that appeared to have two boxes in it. He kind of smirked when he put it under the tree and his wife Jen was giving him the look that said, "You better let her know this was not MY idea!!" After dinner we sat down in the living room and Matthew wanted his gift to us to be first and insisted that I be the one to open it. So I sat down in the middle of our living room and opened the garbage bag. Inside were two unopened boxes that appeared to hold toilet seats. My brain was thinking, "This has to be a joke, right??" But my face was desperately trying to say, "Well, isn't that nice! They got us toilet seats for Christmas!" At this point my husband Larry became very interested and proceeded to open one of the boxes placing the seat on the floor for all to admire. I should mention here that these were not ordinary toilet seats. Nope! They have advanced technology including "whisper-close" lids which means they gently close. Just a nudge of the hand and no slamming (or closing when you least expect it)! Every guy just went, "Wait! What? That right there's a game changer! And every lady has the same look on her face that I did!" My family, being who they are, finished off this part of the gift giving with a number of "toity" jokes which I will not repeat here. But it was actually our four year old granddaughter Lily who stole the show by backing into the one toilet seat on the floor and trying to sit on it. (Apparently humor runs in this family!) My oldest, Michael, completely lost it as did the rest of us! There really is never a dull moment in Jackie's World but this one was a slam dunk!
#sortofbecauseitdoesntslam#anypottyinastorm#3sons2toiletseatsendless-toityjokes

*L*AST WEEKEND LARRY AND I MET OUR DAUGHTER-IN-LAW JEN AND GRANDDAUGHTER Lily for supper at Wendy's. Lily was being her typical almost five year old self and showing me funny sounds she could make, faces she could create and a nice little run across the room to show me her incredible speed! I told Lily if she ate all of her dinner I had a surprise for her. She ate every bit and then came to me to search my purse. There is a candy treat called Kinder Joy that has a delicious chocolate cream candy (I'll explain how I know that in a second) on one side and a little toy on the other. In my purse in a baggie was half of a Kinder Joy….the toy half. Lily took it out and went to her seat and began to pull it out of the baggie. She was looking at the toy and a puzzled expression crossed her face. I said, "Oh, sorry Lily! Gramma ate the candy!" (Okay…don't judge! I had one of these things left over since Christmas and curiosity just got the best of me! At least I saved the toy for her!) Lily's face changed instantly and not into one of the cute faces she made before. Her eyebrows shot right up into her hair line, her eyes popped wide open, she lowered her chin slightly and she questioned me without saying a word! She didn't have to! Her "look" said it all! "You're joking, right Gramma? Seriously…where's the candy?" I knew immediately I had a crossed a Gramma/grandchild line! What was I thinking? Well, the week before I was thinking how good that candy looked! Her mom glanced towards me and discreetly said, "Miss Jackie…..you might have led with that!" Yes, I might have. And I learned my lesson! If you eat the candy, for Heaven's sake, keep the toy!!

#nevertakecandyfromachild#butthechocolatewassogood
#grammasarejustkidsingrownupbodies#andtheyhavenowillpower

WHEN MY GRANDKIDS WERE LITTLE I LIKED TO HELP THEM USE THEIR IMAGINATION. We had rainy day picnics upstairs in a bedroom complete with a picnic basket and a blanket when the weather was bad. One time I told Elliott and Brynn that I knew where there was a T-rex hiding and I took them to a house on the lake that had all their trees shrouded in heavy burlap. One tree in particular had an odd shape and looked very much like a dinosaur. I'm not sure they believed that one but it sure did make them smile! Another day Elliott told me he wanted to be a secret agent. So he borrowed an old brief case from Papa, I managed to put a tie on him, he put on his sunglasses and strolled down our block, brief case in hand, looking like Mr. Cool. And he was convinced a few people thought he was with the Secret Service! When Ariel visited from Arizona where she hardly ever sees rain, I gave her my bright yellow umbrella and she danced in the drops of a rainstorm. And more recently when everyone was here for Christmas, Lily Bean's two girl cousins managed to convince her that they had accidentally turned her invisible. Ariel and Brynn came and got me and let me in on the game. When I came upstairs there sat Lily in a chair absolutely still literally thinking I couldn't see her. And I looked right at her and said to the other girls, "What have you done with Lily? I can't find her!" Lily smiled with delight! (This also proved to be a very effective way to keep Beans quiet for quite a long time!) Why do I do this? Because it's good to have an imagination. It's beautiful to see the delight in a child's eyes! (Especially when you're looking right at them and they think you can't see them!) And because we need a little bit more of this in our lives. We all carry burdens that are sometimes heavy and a bit of imagination and some smiles and laughter do wonders to lift that load. So think about it. And the next time you see someone's trees covered for the winter…see if you can figure out what kind of dinosaur it is! Apparently there's a T-rex that has a fondness for Lake Michigan!!!

I HAVE AN IHOME ALARM CLOCK. I'M NOT SURE IF IT'S A "SMART" CLOCK BUT I DO know it's smarter than me. It's a very nice clock with approximately a dozen buttons on top of it. I know how to use three! Alarm one, alarm two and snooze. Sunday night when I was making sure the alarm was set for Monday morning I accidentally hit the wrong button and the radio started playing. I couldn't figure out how to turn it off! My first plan of attack was to look at the manual which said absolutely nothing about how to turn anything off! Next I hit the three buttons I know how to use. Nothing! After that I decided to stare at it very sternly hoping I could intimidate it to stop. That didn't work either. And finally I threw myself face down on the bed and whined a little. (Okay a lot and I might have cussed once!) That was absolutely no help and now I was becoming "alarmed" that the music was going to play all night. Finally I knew I had to pull out the big guns and I climbed the stairs to the second floor where Larry was having his usual Sunday night phone conversation with his mom. I got his attention and asked, "Would you please ask your mom if you could call her back in a few minutes. I (whimper) need your help." (My apologies mom but desperate times call for desperate measures!) He asked what was going on. And, in full meltdown mode, I cried, "I pushed the wrong button on my alarm clock and now it won't stop playing!!!" He came downstairs with me, picked up the manual I had set aside and within minutes the music stopped. "How?", I asked. His response? "I hit the power button." (You could literally HEAR my eyes roll!) Really?? The POWER button!! Bottom line...smart person...ONE! Smart clock...ZERO! At least until the next time I hit the wrong button!
#larryisasmartman#hecanfixasmartclock#buthehasnoideawhattodoin-akitchen

ONE MORNING I WAS MAKING THE BED AND FOUND WHAT LOOKED LIKE A RED ball just peeking out from under the bedspread. I picked it up to look at it and discovered it was actually an old, plastic, red apple.....with teeth marks in it! And that made me smile! Now let me take you back more than 20 years ago to the time when we had a 120 pound yellow lab named Opie. I also had a basket of the afore mentioned apple (minus the teeth marks) and grandkids who spent Wednesdays at my house. The kids loved to play with those apples and Opie loved to grab any that rolled onto the floor and run with it through the house until he lost it or I caught him! And now let's come back to the present morning. One where I needed something that would lift my spirit a little bit. An old, plastic, red apple rolling out from under my bed did just the thing. Because I was suddenly transported back to the time of children playing with apples in my kitchen, a beloved pet taking them and running with them, and me chasing him around the house trying to get them back! I learned two things from this moment. One; apparently I have not cleaned under my bed in a number of years!! Two; sometimes God will give you a memory when you least expect it but really need it. A little piece of your long ago will roll right into your mind and you'll remember a good thing, a special moment, a cherished time. Opie's been gone many years now. He laughed with us (seriously, he could grin and occasionally said, "Ha!"), he cried with us (he refused to leave my side if I was upset about anything), and he loved his family big. We all have days when we need a smile. In fact God tells us to dwell on those things that are lovely and of good report. Finding Opie's apple that morning released a floodgate of lovely feelings that helped carry me through my day. So let memories live in your heart, be thankful that God saved them for you. And once in a while let one of them roll out from beneath your burdens and get found on your face in a smile of remembrance! And then let it carry you through your day!

I WOKE UP YESTERDAY MORNING REMEMBERING SOMETHING I HAVEN'T THOUGHT about in years. When I was very young I had rheumatic fever. It came from strep throat and it had settled in my heart. I spent almost an entire year either in the hospital or bedridden at home. I remember wanting to be able to go outside and play like the other kids but I couldn't because of the risk to my health. When I was finally healthy part of my continued medical care included a once a month injection of a very potent antibiotic. It had to be refrigerated and so was cold, thick and very painful when injected. I can remember my nurse. She had red hair and her name was Kay and she was so kind to me. I would count to 10 as she did the injection When it was all over she would very carefully remove the needle from the syringe, wash it clean, and give me the empty syringe as my reward for enduring the pain. (They made rather unique squirt guns!) It no longer had the medicine in it. It could no longer hurt me. And in that moment I felt like I had won a victory! One more injection down. I wondered why that memory had popped into my head. And then I remembered what time of year it is and thought maybe the Lord was reminding me of the pain His Son endured on His path to the cross. Pain like I will never ever be able to completely understand. And His reward was an empty tomb. It had been carefully cleaned, washed by the blood of the Lamb, no longer able to bring hurt or pain. And He did win a victory...over sin and death. And unlike my monthly injections, Jesus did this once for all for those who would believe. And now we can be healed, saved, whole because of the pain He endured...because of the empty tomb!

*L*AST NIGHT WE HAD THE PLEASURE OF AN OVERNIGHTER WITH BEANS. SO LET ME tell you about sleeping with a five year old in your bed. It's a misconception. There IS no sleeping with a five year old in your bed. To begin with, just as I'm ready to turn the lights off, she closes her eyes, tilts her head back and starts singing. Must have been her evening lullaby! 🎵🎵 And you know the meme that says something about sleeping with a toddler is like sleeping with a drunk octopus? Nailed it! Seriously, legs and arms everywhere! I spent most of the night confined to 12 inches while Beans owned the rest of our queen size bed! About 6:30 I noticed she was missing. And I'm like…..great, I lost her!! I looked around and found her standing at the end of the bed. I said, "Lily it's not time to get up yet." She got back into bed and said, "Okay Gramma." I thought she was all settled in hopefully for maybe another hour and then she snuggled up against me and kissed me right in the ear and said, "I love you Gramma!" And now I don't care that I've been up most of the night because my heart is full and my ear is wet! I woke up about 8:00 and went out to the living room. She followed soon after and crawled up into my lap and wrapped her little self around me. A few minutes later she got out of my lap and went to the kitchen. She came back with a purple jelly bean that we had set aside the night before for her to have today. And now that she had warmed me up with kisses and hugs and bunches of love could I tell her no to one jelly bean for breakfast?? Pffttt…..not gonna happen! Besides, she needed something to hold her over until I could get her unicorn pop tart warmed up. (And just so you know, I also cut up some grapes to go with that jelly bean and pop tart so….ha!) And there you have it….the breakfast of champions for a five year old! At least at Gramma's!! So our overnighter was a success! She survived, I survived, it was a win/win!! (And, yes, I had jelly beans as well!)

W E STOPPED BY OUR SON MATTHEW'S HOUSE A FEW WEEKS AGO. WHEN WE GOT there he was upstairs changing out of his work clothes. When he came down no one noticed him except his wife Jen. She kind of laughed and said, "Well, look at that! It's Mark!" Mark is Matthew's identical twin brother. And Matthew was wearing the same type of t-shirt that Mark always wears and without his glasses on he did, in fact, look just like Mark. (Again, identical twins!) Our granddaughter Lily ran to her daddy and he picked her up and hugged her and then Matthew took his usual spot on the couch. Lily, however, was watching him quite intently. And then she unexpectedly ran over and jumped in Matthew's lap. She hugged him again and then sat back and said rather sheepishly, "Are you my daddy??" Apparently she really was confused as to whether this was her daddy or her uncle! In her defense we had been talking about her Uncle Mark's upcoming visit and she didn't actually see if anyone came in the door with us. But here's the thing. When she looked into her daddy's eyes (or uncle's) she saw love. When he hugged her she felt loved. And when she asked if he was her daddy, his reply was, "Of course I am!" And you know what? That's the way it should be in a family. Love without question even when we're not so alike. And how much more so in the family of God! When your brother or sister in Christ looks at you, you should see love. When they hug you, you should feel loved. And one day you will see your Heavenly Father face to face and you'll climb up in His lap like a little child and ask, "Are you my Father?" And He will say, "Of course I am! Now go on over there and hug your brothers and sisters. They've been waiting for you! Oh, and not all of you are exactly alike. But it's okay. We're all family!!" #immatthewhesmark#immarkhesmatthew#theyoncetoldmetheywere- clones

*M*AY WAS AN EVENTFUL MONTH FILLED WITH FAMILY TIME, LONG WEEKENDS, getaways and, yes, it was all about me! Until it was time to renew my driver's license. I suddenly became a nobody...literally! Larry and I were getting ready to take our trip up north to Jackie's World and I decided to renew my license before we left. I wanted to get the new real ID so I came prepared with all my appropriate records including my original, green, stamped and embossed birth certificate. I waited my turn in line and eventually got to the counter where a young lady began to enter my information in her computer. She stopped with a puzzled look on her face and asked if this was my correct birth date. Yes. Was this the correct county I was born in. Yes. Did my parents change my name after I was born. Um... no! As the questions continued I realized there was a problem. The real question was am I me...yes! Can I prove it...apparently not!! The State of Michigan had no record of my birth! I asked how this could possibly happen. She replied, "Well, sometimes they update the system and some things get missed." For 65 years? She said she would have to fax the State and would probably have it corrected in a few hours. Because we were going out of town she said she could have the paperwork faxed to another office in the area where we were heading. She gave me a special red ticket so I could go directly to the front of the line when we got there. And so we headed north to Jackie's World. I contacted the boys right away and let them know about the current situation. You know, my being an illegal resident and all, and assured them that I would call as soon as it was safe to do so. The following day we crossed over the Mighty Mac to St Ignace, a beautiful little town with some of our favorite shopping stops AND a Secretary of State office. We arrived at the office, red ticket in hand, to find one counter, one employee, and absolutely no one else in the place. I stood in the non-existent line and held up my special red ticket which made the young lady behind the counter laugh. And you know what! She knew EXACTLY who I was! I never even had to say my name! She took care of my license in short order and I once again was "somebody" in the State of Michigan. It didn't really matter to me anyway. We were in Jackie's World and I was already wearing the crown! So ha!!

*I*SEE A VARIETY OF ROAD KILL ON MY DRIVE TO AND FROM WORK BUT NOTHING HAS surprised me more than the Canadian goose lying on the side of the road. It was flat on its back with its wings sprawled straight out on either side. And I have to say, it begged a number of questions. To begin with, who hits a goose on a busy highway? Or did it just fall from the sky? Was it trying to cross the street? And if so why? Was it the goose that laid the golden egg? I would think that might be quite tiring! So did it simply faint or possibly lie down to rest? Because it wasn't there on my drive home. I think I like that answer. And I'm going to further hypothesize and say that it was a female (because no guy can understand the kind of tired that makes you flop down anywhere just to breathe) and she had littles that she was trying to guide safely across the street. When she finally got them all to the other side she passed out from sheer exhaustion and stress! Her babies were probably secure under her wings. Yes, that's what I choose to believe. So now I have one more question on my mind. Do you ever feel that way? Stressed, tired, just needing to let yourself rest awhile. (Preferably not on the side of a busy highway!) Then do it! When life, kids, jobs, etc have worn you to a frazzle lay yourself down, spread out your arms and just rest awhile. And when you're ready, rise up, lift your arms and fly like the creature God created you to be secure in the fact that His wings will cover you, His heart will guide you, and His love will sustain you…through it all! And let me say just one more thing. If you are ever traveling on a busy highway and you happen to see a goose trying to get to the other side with her babies, for Heaven's sake, slow down and let her cross! Better yet, pull over and offer her a ride because if she is the golden egg laying goose that might just work in your favor! Just sayin……….

Jacqualine K. Boog

W E HAVE A LITTLE GUY THAT COMES TO OUR CHURCH WITH HIS FAMILY. HE HAS an ailment that causes him to put anything and everything in his mouth. For that reason we take necessary precautions in our nursery to prevent him from putting something in his mouth that he could swallow. And I should probably add, he is also extremely fast. One Sunday a few weeks ago one of our nursery attendants was called into unexpected duty. She willingly agreed to fill an empty spot completely forgetting that she was wearing a bracelet made of marble beads. And you guessed it; this little boy got hold of it and before she knew it the elastic broke and beads were rolling all over the floor in front of her while he was reaching for every one. She couldn't actually pick him up before he got his hands on any. So she did the next best thing. She got him flat on the ground and covered his body with her own at the same time grabbing as many beads as she could before he did! High five to my nursery tending friend! She literally lost her marbles yet remained in control! She gave no thought to her own situation. I mean, seriously, I can't imagine how ridiculous that looked. She laid herself down for another to keep him from harm! And isn't that what the Good Book says? "Greater love has no one than this, than to lay down one's life (self) for another." And isn't that exactly what Christ did for us? He took no thought of Himself and covered our lives with His own to keep us from harm. There used to be a saying. WWJD. What would Jesus do? But I'd like to ask a different question. WWYD. What would YOU do? Would you be willing to lay yourself down for another? Would you be willing to look ridiculous to keep another from harm? Would you be willing to be more like the one Who created you to be like Him? I would! So if you ever see me flat on the floor on my face, first check to see if there's a child underneath me that I'm protecting from harm. Then make sure I haven't lost my marbles! Because in my life, that's more likely the case!

WE WERE AT MCDONALD'S WITH OUR GRANDDAUGHTER LILY AND HER MOM AND dad the other night and Lily wanted to sit next to me. So I scooted over and she scooted down towards me. I scooted again and she scooted closer. And I wondered how much room does this little girl need? I scooted one more time and down she came until she was right next to me. The thing was she wanted to be close enough to touch me. As we were eating she began to share her secrets with me. One of them was her password. I asked what the password was for. She said it was for her secret place. Now I can't share that password with you but I will say that if Lily did not love her Gramma very, very much she would never be able to get inside her secret place! As we were finishing up I told her I had something in my purse for her when she was done eating. And when she had eaten the last bite I let her look in my purse. She found two Kinder Joys. I told her that one was for her and one was for me. She chose the one she wanted and then I said, "Lily, I love you so much that I am going to give you mine!" Her eyes got big and her grin went from ear to ear and she said, "And I'm going to give you mine!" Oh. My. Heart! Now my son Matthew has always said I "Jesus-ize" his daughter with my stories. He's right. I do! And I will continue to do so until this little girl stops showing me the world through a child's eyes. From the innocence of her heart she preached a three point sermon right there in McDonald's! Point #1: Scoot and keep scooting. Take all the room you need until you're as close to God as you can get! Point #2: In order to enter God's secret place you need to be willing to share your innermost secrets and express your love towards Him. And #3: Share your (Kinder) joy! Give to others just as they have given to you! There it is folks. Out of the mouth of a babe, placed in the heart of a Gramma, and "Jesus-ized" into a story for you! Thank you Lily Bean for reminding me of the simple intricacies of the love of God!

*M*Y OLDEST SON MICHAEL RECENTLY HAD NECK SURGERY. IT WAS THE FIRST surgery he's ever had. He is healing great, prognosis is excellent, and the surgery itself was very successful. Except for one thing. After the surgery the doctor came out to tell us that everything had gone fine and the nurse would be out in about 30 minutes to take us back to see Michael. An hour and a half later we were still waiting. His wife, Tami, and I were getting very concerned so we started trying to find somebody to tell us what was going on. The front desk got hold of post-op and sent a nurse out who explained to us that Michael was fine. But here's where the problem occurred. Apparently my son does not come out of anesthesia very well. He woke up kicking, flailing, pulling tubes, punching and all while wearing a neck brace. It took FIVE people to restrain him so they could re-sedate him and calm him down. As they were waking him up again, this time a little slower, the nurse was tapping on his chest and asking, "Mike. Mike. Do you know what day it is?" In his anesthesia stupor he replied, "Hump day?" (That's my boy!) Now flash back to sometime in 1982. A five year old boy leads his mom into the bathroom, closes the door, turns off the light, and says, "Look Mom!" "At what?" she questions. "My eyes", the child says. "Can you see them? They are glowing! And they're green!" Mmmmm. Now many years later let me put this all together for you. Glowing green eyes, incredibly strong when frightened, and a bit of a comedian. I think what we have here is proof positive that.....I GAVE BIRTH TO THE HULK! I've got to say I'm pretty impressed by that. I mean…go figure! So fear not our local metropolis! We are safe from evil villains! And you're welcome!

I TURNED A CORNER AT WORK AND WALKED DOWN THE HALLWAY AT THE SAME TIME a patient came out of a room behind me. She called a name that wasn't mine so I kept walking. She called the same name again so I checked my name tag just to be sure and then turned to look at her. She said, "Oh, you're not (still not my name). You look just like her. She is an amazing human being and you have that same twinkle!" Well, praise God and hallelujah! I got me a twinkle! Not sure what that is but it made a difference in this lady's life because I look like someone special to her and that made her smile AND it made me smile! And somehow we each felt a little better after that encounter because there is something comforting about finding a familiar trait in another. Now, you have got to know where I'm going with this. Aren't we created in the image of our Heavenly Father? And shouldn't people see something in us (a twinkle perhaps) that reminds them of goodness and love? There is no doubt that we are amazing human beings because He made us that way. (Some versions of the Bible also say we are peculiar but I'll save that for another day!) He also made us to love, to bring joy, and to live to be more like Him. So it shouldn't surprise us when someone looks our way and, even in mistaking us for someone else, still finds something comforting in us because we remind them of someone special in their lives. So be the person He created you to be, make a difference in someone's life, smile along with them, and go out there and let your twinkle shine!

#twinkletwinklelittlestarandthealphabetsongarethesame
#ijustmadeyousingbothsongs#twinkling

*I*AM GOING TO TELL YOU TWO THINGS BEFORE I START MY STORY. FIRST, I BOUGHT a Fitbit and I love it. I find it is not always completely accurate as it thought I was swimming Saturday morning. I did some laundry but I did NOT get in the washer. I did, however, get points for exercise so… ha! Second, we had the most beautiful service Sunday morning. It was a time of God's love, His power, and His promises. Now let me put the two together. At some point during the time of extended worship I felt my wrist begin to tingle. At first I thought, "Is that you Lord?" I glanced down and realized my Fitbit was informing me that I had met and exceeded my 10,000 steps for the day! Fireworks were going off and stars were shining! I discovered later that it thought I was riding a bike as I was leading worship so I received congratulations for exercising and some kind of badge for being an overachiever! From my perspective it was a win/win situation. A two-fer if you will. A spiritual AND a physical victory! I guess I take my walk with the Lord quite seriously! And so it should be with all of us. Because the Bible tells us to "lay aside every weight, and the sin which so easily ensnares us, and run with endurance the race that is set before us." So walk with the Lord in a determined way, take it seriously, and make every step count! And one day fireworks will go off, stars will shine and we'll hear the words we long for…"Well done good and faithful overachiever!" As for me, when I got home that afternoon I decided a nap was in order because what was left to do? I had met with the Lord, I had met my daily steps, and I had met good friends for lunch! Besides, the Word also tells us that the young will see visions and the old will dream dreams! Just sayin……..

I LOVE THE FALL. IT'S PROBABLY ONE OF MY FAVORITE SEASONS WITH THE LOVELY colors, the wonderful smells, the delicious apples! But there is one thing that comes with this changing season that I do not like and that is creepy, crawly things that think our house is warmer than the air outside. And such was the case the other night. I was just about ready for bed and went to the kitchen for a drink of water when…I saw it. A huge, brown spider on my bare, cream colored wall! It was practically casting a shadow! And I'm going to take a wild guess and say that its leg span was at least 2-3 inches! I stopped in my tracks not wanting to cause it to scamper away and began to wave my hands and whisper loudly to Larry who was in the living room. "Larry! Larry! A spider! A spider! It's huge! It's huge!" Apparently I thought by repeating everything twice he would understand the magnitude of the situation. He did not. But he did get the gist of what I was implying and came to my rescue. When he saw the culprit he shooed me back in the bedroom and assured me he'd get it. However, what I saw in his eyes was, "Wow! She's actually right this time! That IS a huge spider!" Now Larry is usually a paper towel guy when it comes to killing spiders but this time he went with the big gun…the flyswatter! I stayed securely behind the closed bedroom door and heard a wack. And then a second wack. And finally a third! And I thought, "No-o-o-o! He's got himself a runner!" At this point everything went silent. I peeked out and asked was it safe. Larry told me it was but I asked the usual questions. Was it dead? Were there any others? Because they travel in pairs; sometimes herds! He said there were no others and, yes, it was definitely dead. The third wack did him in! I thanked him and went back to the kitchen to get that drink of water which for some silly reason I still wanted! As I returned to the bedroom I calmly and confidently said to Larry, "Contact a realtor because we will be moving! That thing had a family and they are NOT going to be happy when he turns up missing!"

A FEW SUNDAYS AGO WE HAD A SPECIAL SERVICE WITH A GUEST MISSIONARY. After the morning worship time I took my place in my usual strategically located seat. Third row back, end chair, easy access to keyboard and exit path from sanctuary. After Pastor Mike introduced the guest speaker he came back to his seat in the row in front of me but for whatever reason he picked it up and placed it right beside me! I looked at him and said, "What are you doing??" He replied, "I'm making sure you're taking good notes!" I smiled but in my head I was saying, "Seriously? I always take good notes! And this is my spot!" So now I'm feeling just a little awkward. I tried to act "natural" but everything I did seemed "unnatural". My normal routine from here is to reward myself with an after worship Werther's caramel candy. I took one out of my purse and couldn't decide if I should offer one to Pastor Mike or just discreetly put it in my mouth. I chose the second but the wrapper made a lot of crinkly noise. Next I took a drink from my water bottle which was making noises like it was going to explode! I sometimes leave the sanctuary for just a minute, usually to get extra music for the end of the service but now I felt like I was stuck there because my exit was blocked. Finally I decided I was being silly. I mean, it wasn't like the Lord Himself was sitting next to me! Hold on! Wait just a minute! What if that were the case? What if Jesus had moved his chair next to mine and was sitting there with me? Would I want to reward myself with a sweet treat or would my reward be the sweetness of His presence? Would I feel awkward about the noise my water bottle made or would I unashamedly use it to wash His feet? And finally, would I even want to move from that spot at all or would I sit at His side for hours and not even know time had passed? Well, that brought things into perspective for me. But Pastor Mike should probably choose his seat wisely. Apparently there are people out there who might randomly throw candy at you or pour water on your feet!

I'D LIKE TO SHARE WITH YOU THE STORY OF HOW MY HUSBAND LARRY AND I MET AND how God always has a plan. It was a little over 35 years ago. I had been left to raise three young boys on my own. I couldn't stay on the military base where we had been living and I had no family there so I packed up our belongings and headed north from Georgia to my hometown in Michigan with twin toddlers and a six year old in our family size van. The one thing I could not "take" with me was my meager savings. I had that wired to a bank in Michigan. And that's where it all started. For whatever reason, my savings did not reach my bank until almost three weeks after my arrival. I would call the bank every, single morning and in my sweetest, southern drawl (I lived in Georgia for some time and adapted easily to their way of speaking!) would ask the manager, "Good morning. This is Mrs. Bennett. Has my money arrived from Georgia yet?" The manager got tired of speaking with me and transferred my calls to the assistant manager, a Mr. Larry Boog. I then spoke with him almost every morning. He apparently didn't get tired of my calls. (Little did he know!) After my savings finally arrived, it became my routine to stop at the bank every Friday night and get my allowance, the money I needed for groceries, etc. And guess who was ALWAYS there at the teller counter? Mr. Larry Boog! But it didn't stop there. I needed to find a job to take care of my family. Guess where they were hiring bank tellers? At the same bank where Mr Larry Boog worked, where we became friends, eventually started dating, fell in love, and became Mr. AND Mrs. Larry Boog! Tomorrow we celebrate our 35th wedding anniversary. God always has a plan!! So that's my story, about a lovely lady, who was bringing up three young boys on her own. Until one day she met a fella........ Wait a minute. Wrong story! I love you Larry! Thank you for making my family your own, for helping me raise three fine young men, and for doing life with me with grace and love through it all!

#wearenotthebradybunch#ididnothaveamaid#butididhaveahunchabout-thisbunch

#wearefamily#nowyouhavetwosongsstuckinyourhead

Jacqualine K. Boog

*H*AVE YOU EVER HAD A SONG STUCK IN YOUR HEAD AND NOT BE ABLE TO FIGURE out what it is? Well that's exactly what happened to our church guitarist, Tom. He came in on a Sunday morning for practice, sat down in his chair, and began to play a song. I said, "What's that?" He said, "I don't know." "Is it a church song?", I asked. "Nope. I'm thinking rock-n-roll", he replied. And based on what he was playing I agreed. 1960's maybe with an Elvis feel. We could both hum the tune but neither one of us could figure out what the name of the song was. And let me just add that there is nothing funnier than two musicians who can't figure out what song they are playing/singing. We continued our practice for church with Tom playing his unknown song in between most of our worship songs because it was still stuck in his head! And finally we practiced our offering song for the day which was "How Great Thou Art". We ran through it a couple of times and then just sort of stopped and enjoyed the sweet worship we were in. And in that quiet moment, out of nowhere, it came to me and I started singing the "elusive" song! I had the lyrics, Tom started playing along, and we both hit the title line together…"A Crazy Little Thing Called Love"!! Now I'm sure you're wondering how I could come out of a beautiful, sacred hymn and go right into an Elvis rock-n-roll song. (I will admit it was not my finest spiritual moment and my apologies to those who witnessed my victory dance!) Well, I have a couple of possible theories on this. 1. Technically they are both songs about love. Am I right? 2. My mind does not work like the average person. I'll make no other comments on that subject! But a third possibility is this….when I think about How Great He is I realize how "crazy" in love with Him I am! So in my mind it was apparently a good mash up of songs! Oh, and one more thing. Could you not mention to Pastor Mike that we sometimes practice rock-n-roll songs on Sunday morning? As Elvis would say, "Thank ya. Thank ya very much!"

Around Thanksgiving Larry and I went to our granddaughter Lily's kindergarten grandparent's day. We arrived at the school and were directed to the library where we found a seat (and by seat I mean something the size of a thimble with four legs attached) along with all the other grandparents. Shortly after that our five year olds filed in and began their program of holiday songs. There were, however, two problems. The first was that we couldn't see Lily and she couldn't see us so we decided to stand up and move off to the side. The second was figuring out how to gracefully get out of the thimble sized chair! As soon as we were standing Lily started waving and smiling because we could now see each other. The kids were very excited and after each song we applauded, they applauded, and then they would settle down to get ready for the next song. During one of these quiet times between songs the most beautiful thing happened. Lily unashamedly looked up at me and loudly declared, "I love you Gramma!" There was an audible "Aww!" from every grandparent in the room and I'm sure there were those who were looking to see where this Gramma was. But I had eyes for only Lily. She held my full attention. Through a misty smile I blew her a kiss. And now here it comes…the spiritual application. Because Lily's reactions reminded me again of how much our heavenly Father loves us. He will search and not be satisfied until He can see our faces. In quiet moments he will unashamedly declare His love for us. And He will not be satisfied until He has our full and undivided attention. And on that day when you meet Him face to face and He says, "Welcome child. I have prepared a place for you.", tell Him how much you love Him and ask Him please if you could have a BIG chair to go with your mansion! #Jesuslovesyou#lilyloveshergramma#seriouslysmallchairs

*M*OST SUNDAYS PASTOR MIKE WILL CALL ME TO COME BACK TO THE PLATFORM following his message to lead in a last song. And this was exactly the case a few weeks ago. Or so I thought. Mike had been preaching on wisdom and knowledge and he had made some very good points. As he was beginning to wind down he asked a question that went something like this, "How much knowledge do you have….Jackie?" and then he hesitated. And I thought….what? Is he seriously asking me how smart I am? In front of the entire congregation? For what seemed like a minute and a half but was most likely less than 5 seconds, my mind began to frantically search for the right answer. In my "caught off guard" state the only thing I could think to do was recite the Lord's Prayer. I guess I figured that by the time I got to the "Amen" most people would think we were done and there would be no need for a final song OR an answer to Mike's question. And just as I was about to start the "Our Father" Mike finished his question with, "Will you come and lead us in one more song?" Whew!! Crisis averted! There was a collective sigh of relief from most, including myself. But there were also a few looks of disappointment as some were actually interested in knowing just how much knowledge I have as over the years I have proven myself to be a little lacking in that area, you know, being the resident blonde and all. So IF that would have been Mike's question and IF it would have been necessary to give an answer my response would have been to say nothing. Because I know it seems silly but maybe you all don't need to know how much I know or don't know! Know what I mean?

*I*WORK IN A MEDICAL OFFICE AND ALTHOUGH I DON'T HAVE DIRECT CONTACT WITH patients I am required to wear a mask. One of my co-workers made headbands with buttons using ribbon and an elastic ponytail holder to help with our masks. I decided to try it out. My first attempt was to put the stretchy part under my chin and pull the ribbon over my head. Not a great idea unless what you are going for is a face lift! It soon became apparent that either this headband was a little small or my head is way too big! I was now becoming a great source of entertainment for the staff and so began the suggestions. Someone said to put it on top of my head and sort of work it into place. No luck with that approach because I got it just above my eyebrows when it slowly began to inch its way back up pushing my hair with it! I could hear some snickers so I looked in the window that separates my cubby from the one next to mine and realized I now looked like I was wearing the royal crown… of a TROLL village! Round one of laughter! The maker of the headband came back to our office, took one look at me, and said as only she can, "Oh My Lanta Jackie! What are you doing?" Which started the second round of uncontrollable laughter! She instructed me to remove my glasses, which had become useless from the tears and mascara running down my cheeks, and pull the headband down over my head. Then she said to pull it back over my face and to the top of my head. Again, let me remind you, tight headband, big head. This time it took everything in its path with it! My cheeks, my earrings, my ears and finally my bangs leaving me looking like a child who's pigtails are pulled too tight! And this produced the third and final round of deep belly laughing that left each of us out of breath, with no mascara left, and wishing we had not been trying to stay hydrated! I've read that laughter is an immune booster to which I say…. you're welcome. When I first started working there I told the ladies eventually they would end up in one of my stories so congratulations and welcome to Jackie's World! #comicrelief#iraisedboys#theydidntwearheadbands

(Addendum. This was written during the pandemic in the spring of 2020 when masks had been mandated. It was not meant to make light of all that happened. It was meant to bring laughter in a place where it was very much needed.)

Jacqualine K. Boog

S EVERAL WEEKS AGO ON OUR EVENING WALK I SPOTTED A SWEATSHIRT IN THE WINDOW of a local shop. I really admired it and was pretty sure it would make a great addition to my wardrobe and even mentioned that it would make a nice Mother's Day gift. Well Mother's Day came and went and so did my sweatshirt. I honestly forgot about it until a few weeks later when we were getting ready to go on our bi-annual trip up north to Jackie's World. This wasn't our usual trip because our four day, three night getaway became two day trips. The hotel we have been staying in for about 30 years was unable to open this time as were many of the places we know and love. The morning of our first day trip I found myself getting angry. I felt like something had been taken from me. That I had been robbed of something important to my life. This trip has always been a breath of fresh air for me. A place where I feel like I can finally relax, regroup, and center myself. As I was getting dressed I just couldn't find anything to wear that felt right (ladies you know what I'm talking about) and I was starting to get a bit of an attitude. While still in my pajamas I went to Larry and I whined, "You know what would make this day just a little bit better for me? Having that sweatshirt I saw to wear up north." I went back to the bedroom, finished dressing, and in walked Larry with a beautifully wrapped box in his hand and declared, "Happy early birthday!" I sat on the bed, took the lid off, and there was my sweatshirt. I could barely speak but managed to say, "I can't believe you did this!" And then I began to cry. I stood up and hugged him and then he started to cry. But here's the thing, my tears were not just for the sweatshirt. My tears were for the things that I felt had been taken away from me. For the changes in my life that I don't deal with very well. (Those of you who really know me, stop laughing!) For a trip that had to be altered and would not be the same this time. But then I realized something else. Maybe it's not about the things we want or think we need. Maybe it's about spending time with our loved ones however that looks. And maybe it's about giving and receiving. And maybe, just maybe, at the end of the day. . . . . it's about taking your wife to Clyde's drive in for supper Which locals will know is both a need and a want and best when shared with those you love!
#mushroomswissburger#blt#onionrings
#cherrymalt#perfectday

I HAVE A FRIEND WHO LIVES UP NORTH. HE AND HIS WIFE HAVE AN INTENSE LOVE and passion for dogs, especially rescue dogs. Earlier this week Dave's wife saw a notification on Facebook about a rescue dog that escaped from the new owner's car while she was at a gas station. They immediately went to the area where the dog went missing. They could see the little guy but he was afraid, lost, and very skittish. So they just hung out there with him, keeping their distance and watching. They were very concerned as coyotes had been seen in this area, it was near a major highway, and the weather was very iffy. The next day Dave went back again. It was the same scenario as he let this lost pup get used to him being around. He was still not able to get near him but the dog knew someone was there and that someone cared. What happened on the third attempt to win this dog over was what brought me to tears. Dave spent hours with him on this day and was finally able to get close. And as he did he literally laid down on the ground a few feet from the dog. He quietly and calmly remained there letting the pup get used to his presence and trust him. Every couple of minutes he would slowly push the leash towards him letting him sniff it and eventually, very gently, was able to wrap it around the dog and get him to safety. I'm going to tell you that I feel a lot like that lost pup right now. I'm uncertain, worried, not sure which way to turn. But when I heard about this act of kindness I was reminded about the love of the Great Shepherd for His sheep. For He will go to any extreme to protect the one that is lost. He will calmly and quietly lay Himself down next to you and wait for you to get used to His presence. And when he feels you are comfortable and willing to trust He will ever so gently reach out and wrap His loving arms around you and carry you to safety; out of the storms, away from predators and protected from harm. So thank you Dave for being a dog whisperer and watching over this lost one. Thank you Jesus that all I have to do is whisper your name and I know You are watching over me.

Jacqualine K. Boog

I HAD A BIT OF AN ISSUE LAST WEEKEND AS I WAS GETTING READY FOR MY DAY. I WAS doing my hair using my normal arsenal of tools including root lifter, mousse, gel, texture spray, blow dryer and blow brush. (Hey…it takes a village, okay!) While using the blow brush is where everything came to a screeching halt. This appliance is basically an electric brush which dries and styles at the same time. I somehow got the blow brush tangled in the back of my hair and I could not get it to release its grip. I turned it off and unplugged it from the outlet to try and get a better assessment of the situation. But there didn't seem to be any way to get my hair removed from it. I very briefly considered scissors and then came to my senses before anything drastic happened! So with the brush firmly attached to my head and the cord dangling behind me I set out to find my husband Larry. He was fortunately in a nearby room. I walked through the door and tried to say, "Please don't laugh" but at this point I realized how ridiculous I looked and lost it! I couldn't stop laughing nor could I speak! And by the look on his face I'm pretty sure that ship had sailed anyway! I did manage to say, "I'm stuck!" which I'm pretty sure he had already figured out. He told me to stand still and he very gently removed the brush from the power handle. With that being done he was able to slowly remove the tangled hair one tiny piece at a time. And praise God hallelujah I was free!!! I finished up and went downstairs. Shortly after Larry came to me and sincerely said, "I just wanted to tell you it was really nice to hear you laugh." Aww! And I'll be honest, I'm just a little impressed that he could rescue me from a hair appliance! As I thought about writing this story I tried to find a spiritual application. You know, like how God helps us through the "tangles" in our lives. Or patience is a virtue. Laughter is the best medicine. But I decided to go with Matthew 10:30 which says, "The very hairs on your head are numbered." And all I'll say about that is it's a good thing that strands 2,988 through 3,050 were being watched over because they came very close to being separated from the rest of the "flock". And I for one would have missed them!

$\mathcal{S}$EVERAL WEEKS AGO I WAS DAYDREAMING AND A SONG CAME INTO MY HEAD. I knew every note. I knew every word. And I know where it came from. It was my mom's favorite song. She used to sing it in the car when we were coming back from my grandma's house in a neighboring town. I remember being in the passenger seat beside her. I remember the scarf she tied around her hair. I remember her red lipstick. Mom always wore lipstick. And so do I but usually not red. And I remember singing the song with her. I didn't know it then but I followed her lead and we sang together............

"I'm forever blowing bubbles, pretty bubbles in the air

They fly so high nearly reach the sky then like my dreams they fade and die.

Fortunes always hiding, I've looked every where

I'm forever blowing bubbles. Pretty bubbles in the air."

When mom sang that song she sang it with feeling. As a child I watched her. As an adult I can understand why this song touched her. Because mom had dreams that faded. She wanted more for her family. She wanted the best. But it didn't always happen. That didn't stop her from "blowing bubbles" and trying to make the best of each situation. Which is where some of us are right now. We are facing situations that are not exactly what we were hoping for. Dreams have faded and we continue to "look everywhere" for the answers. Well, my heart knows where the answers are but I can't always get my head to wrap around that. And so I get worried and concerned about everything when really it's as simple as "blowing bubbles". It's called release. A giving of your concerns, letting them go to the only One that can carry them for you. And He will! That's His promise to us. In fact, He has already been where you need to be. So let's keep singing, let's keep hoping, let's keep blowing bubbles. Besides, seriously, what's funnier than a bunch of baby boomers blowing bubbles! Pretty bubbles in the air!

*I*THOUGHT I LOST ONE OF MY FAVORITE NECKLACES. IT'S A LIGHT GREEN BEACH GLASS pendant that hangs from a black leather cord. It was a gift from previous employers many years ago and is still one of my go to pieces of jewelry. I unhooked the latch to put it around my neck and somehow lost my grip on one end of the cord and the beach glass fell off. I heard a clink sound and the only thing nearby was the metal heat vent in the bottom part of the wall of our bedroom. I looked all over the floor, ran my hands over the carpet, and checked a container of Mega Blocks that were nearby and found nothing. So I called for help. I explained to Larry what had happened. He moved the nightstand and could not find it under there and then looked at the heat vent and back at me and I said, "No! Please tell me it did not go down the vent!" He said it was possible that's what happened. He went for some kind of tool that guys use for these situations and came back to remove the grate and see if it was on the inside edge. I had been getting lunch ready previous to this and suggested we eat first and while I cleaned up the kitchen he could look further for the beach glass. So we finished lunch and when I was done in the kitchen I went to the bedroom and what I saw was my husband's body crouched on the floor with his entire head in the wall! Which caused me to utter words I never thought I would hear coming from my mouth! "Larry, get your head out of the wall!!" From the wall I heard this response, "Don't tell me what to do!" And as he slowly eased himself out of the vent he also declared, "I'll put my head in the wall if I want to!" I cleverly responded with, "Well, you might want to let your forehead know next time because there's a big, ugly, black smudge on it and it looks angry!" He had the final word with, "Well, maybe I'm observing Ash Wednesday!" (We have the most intelligent conversations of any couple I know!) As he proceeded to search the surrounding area I decided to look one more time in the wagon with the mega blocks but this time just dumped everything out. And as the blocks tumbled out so did my beach glass pendant! I smiled and put on my necklace. Larry smiled and washed his forehead. And since it was Sunday afternoon, we both smiled....and took a nap! It's the little things people! You know, like finding a treasure that was lost, taking a Sunday afternoon nap, getting your husband's head out of the wall. Whatever! It's all good!!

I HAD A BIT OF AN ATTITUDE SATURDAY. IT HAD BEEN A LONG WEEK AND, OH LET'S face it, it's been a long year!! Saturday should have been our annual Applefest which is my very favorite of all the festivals. I guess in comparison it's not all that bad but my world seems to have a lot of bumps in the road lately and Saturday I was angry with just about everybody. (Poor Larry!) So I did my usual Saturday "list" and we decided to visit a few orchards and maybe turn it into a short color tour. As we traveled down the highway the colors just didn't look right. They seemed faded and dull and I complained that they just weren't the same this year. (Like a lot of other things.) We stopped at a local orchard and stood in line, outside, to get a donut that came right out of the fryer, dropped and rolled in cinnamon sugar and then went directly into my mouth! Seriously, Larry took the bag and started walking with it and I said, "What are you doing? Give that to me!" I think he knew the situation was becoming dire and practically hand fed me! It was so good and I started to feel better about things. Apparently a fresh donut is some kind of comfort food for me! We got back on the road and headed south and something strange happened. The colors of the leaves began to pop in hues of red, orange, and yellow. They were vibrant and beautiful and I wondered what made the difference. It was then that I realized that as my attitude changed so did the colors. My outlook changed the atmosphere around me. We finished our drive truly enjoying the sights we were seeing and as we arrived home I had one more realization. The tree with the most beautiful reds, the most vibrant color was right in front of our house. I had been looking at it through eyes that have been dimmed by life's situations and didn't see it's beauty. Wow! Lesson learned! And if you didn't get it I'll share it with you. Think on those things that are just. (That donut was "just" plain good!) Dwell on what is pure. (Pure cinnamon and sugar!) And most importantly, turn your hearts toward home for that is where you will find your treasure.

SUNDAY MORNING DURING WORSHIP TEAM PRACTICE THERE WAS A FLY BUZZING around my head. At first I kept playing and tried to ignore it until it became apparent that its target was my mouth and I was concerned I would inhale it. (As a worship leader I do not want to go down choking on a fly!) My next attempt was to wave it away. Pretty sure it waved back! On its final go around I stopped playing and sort of jumped and clapped my hands above my head and then went right back to my hands on the keyboard. My drummer was laughing, my guitar player was grinning and both were probably thinking, "What is she doing?" In their defense, I kind of looked like I was busting a move….flamingo style! (Our pastor did have a typo a few weeks ago in which he said we were continuing our study in the book of Mariachi instead of Malachi so maybe I was just practicing!) Now there's your laugh for the day but here's something for you to think about. We are all struggling right now in one way or another. For some it runs deep and for others it lays just on the surface affecting everything we do. We can try to ignore our problems. We can try to "wave" them away. We can even try to destroy them with a clap of our hands. But the truth is there is only one answer. His name is Jesus. He was there before this all started, He is with you now in the midst of it, and He will be there when you come out on the other side. And unlike your problems He will not be ignored, He will not be waved away. And the only clapping to be done will be His hands coming together in a mighty sound of thunder. (And FYI… it is not the angels bowling like my parents tried to tell me!) So the choice is yours. You can try to fix all your problems on your own or you can "lean not on your own understanding and in all your ways acknowledge Him." On a side note, I highly recommend a little mariachi dancing. It may not have been my finest musical moment but the look on the faces of my team was definitely worth it!

*M*Y HUSBAND AND I BOTH WORK IN A NEIGHBORING TOWN. SO WE DRIVE together four out of five days or as Larry likes to put it, he's my personal chauffer. He drops me off at my office and then goes down the road a ways to where he works. He gets out a little earlier than I do so he comes back and sits in the waiting room until I'm finished with my day. This has worked perfectly until last week. On Wednesday I was actually ready to leave a little earlier than normal but when I looked for Larry he wasn't there yet. If he has a late delivery or something he usually texts me but I had not heard a thing from him. So I did a few more things, checked again, and he was nowhere to be found. I commented to one of the ladies up front that I couldn't believe he was late and she gently reminded me that he does wait patiently for me each night. Okay, I'll give him that. I decided to gather my stuff and just wait at the back door. Five minutes later still no Larry. So I called him and said, "Where are you?" If I have to be honest it was probably more like, "WHERE! ARE! YOU!" He said he was just coming up the drive and would be right there. I got in the car and we started our 20 minute ride home. And this was where it got interesting as he explained why he was late. He began by telling me that he had to stop for some supplies to fix a clogged drain in our bathroom. He was thinking about how he was going to do this and if he had everything he needed at home. And in his own words, "I was concentrating so hard on my plumbing abilities that I was half way home before I realized you were NOT in the seat next to me!" What? He forgot me!! In his defense he did have a lot on his mind. In my defense, I am unforgettable! There is a message that comes up on the dashboard of the car when you exit that reminds you to check the back seat for occupants. I'm wondering if another reminder could be added that says, "Please check the passenger seat and make sure your wife is there!" The next day the clogged sink was running freely AND he remembered to pick me up after work. So I guess I'll call that a win/win!

*L*ARRY AND I WERE HAVING SUPPER IN THE LIVING ROOM TV TRAY STYLE. (DON'T judge. It's just the two of us and kind of the way we roll lately.) He was watching a game show on TV and I was scrolling through Facebook on my phone when out of nowhere I stopped and shouted, "Macadamia nuts!" He looked up at me with the strangest expression on his face, stopped eating, and then literally laughed out loud! Which is rather unusual for Larry. Not the laughing, the stopping of eating! And he said, "Where on earth did that come from? That's a little over the top even for you!" As a side note…it's not unusual for me to randomly say things that have nothing to do with anything else that's going on. I forget that not everybody else can hear the thoughts going on in my head and I'm easily distracted. I have a co-worker who said she had heard of the "squirrel" phenomenon but had never actually seen it in action until she met me! Later that evening I said to Larry, "You must think I'm losing my mind!" He replied, "No, I just believe there is a lot going on in that mind." And he's right. There is ALWAYS something going on in this mind and sometimes all the thoughts get jumbled up and occasionally one slips out unexpectedly! But at that particular moment what was on my mind was Santa Bags which are our family's version of Christmas stockings and are filled with little things I know my children like. (I once suggested that I might not do them for the adult children anymore and ended up with a mutiny on my hands. And I quote per Matthew, "Ma…I could survive on a deserted island with one of your Santa Bags!) So, for whatever reason, as I was scrolling through Facebook something reminded me that one of my kids really likes, you guessed it, macadamia nuts! Hence, the bursting forth of my proclamation! I can't explain the progression of thoughts that run through my mind. There are few that can! But I will say this. Pay attention to these random outbursts. They could mean something important! Somehow…someday… somewhere! Oh great! Anybody else singing "Somewhere" from West Side Story? No? Just me? Do you see what I mean!!!

I WANTED TO PLAY THE PIANO FROM AS FAR BACK AS I CAN REMEMBER. WHEN I WAS very young my cousin drew an entire keyboard on a long piece of cardboard. I played it like it was real. It never made a sound but I heard the music. Eventually Dad found a piano for me and I started taking lessons from a little old lady. (Old is irrelevant here as she was probably much younger than I am now.) I excelled from the time I started and I'm not sure if that was talent or just a thirst to learn. Eventually I surpassed her ability to teach me and a very good friend introduced me to a new piano teacher, Mary Brown Martin. Mary began to teach me from a higher level. She walked me through four years of musical theory in one year and I started to understand the reasoning behind what I was playing. For the first time I began to read and play classical music, difficult pieces that I worked on for hours, every moment worth the sacrifice. Mary became more than just a teacher. She was my mentor, my friend and sometimes I listener as we talked about matters of the heart. Out of that came the most important thing Mary taught me and that was to put myself into the music. It wasn't enough that I could play the piece well and with confidence. I had to make it mine. Otherwise I was just going through the motions or simply making noise. I would play a song for her and she would say, "That was good. Very good. Now put "Jackie" in it." It was then that I began to feel the music and a new freedom in playing was born. I would know when to linger at a certain spot for emphasis, I could feel the difference in the progression of the chords, and just the touch of my fingers on the keys allowing the music to flow through me took me to higher places musically. And now all these years later as a worship leader I can see how valuable of a lesson this was. Because, as I worship, I know when it's time to linger a bit in His presence. I can feel the difference in the progression of songs to take me closer to Him. And just the touch of His hand on my heart allowing His love to flow through me takes me to higher places spiritually. I learned how to make His song mine. So here's my point especially in these days. Don't just go through the motions. Never just simply make noise. Always let your song be a sweet sacrifice to Him. And remember Mary's words of wisdom; "That was good. Very good. Now put "you" in it." That is the place where you will find freedom, where you can be you and all you were created to be!

Jacqualine K. Boog

*A*S WE HAVE COME TO THE END OF MY STORIES I WOULD LIKE TO LEAVE YOU with some of my favorite pictures from Jackie's World and also a word of explanation. Jackie's World is not just a place I made up. It is, in my opinion, one of God's most beautiful places. It is the area surrounding the Straits of Mackinaw and the Mackinaw Bridge, or as some call it the Mighty Mac, in Northern Michigan and the Upper Peninsula. My husband and I go to this area for a few days a couple of times a year. It has become my happy place. A place where life slows down a little bit, I feel like I can breathe again, and a sense of peace is restored. Several years ago we began to call it Jackie's World because I pretty much reign as queen when we are there! And, seriously, if the crown fits…wear it!

So thank you for purchasing my book and for following me on Facebook where I share most of my stories. Thank you for encouraging me in my musings. And thank you for taking a trip through Jackie's World. I hope the ride was enjoyable!

THE LAKES SURROUNDING MY HOME TOWN.

A BEAUTIFUL SHOT OF OUR LOCAL LIGHTHOUSE AND CHANNEL WITH
TWO FREIGHTERS THAT OFTEN CRUISE THE GREAT LAKES.

ONE OF OUR FAVORITE PHOTO OP PLACES. McGULPIN POINT.

THE FREEZING OF THE GREAT LAKES AND THE SHIFTING OF THE WINDS SOMETIMES CAUSES THIS PHENOMENON. IT'S CALLED BLUE ICE AND TRULY TAKES ON THAT COLOR.

A BEAUTIFUL PICTURE OF THE MIGHTY MAC AND IF YOU LOOK CLOSELY
YOU CAN SEE THAT A FREIGHTER HAS JUST PASSED UNDER THE BRIDGE.

Jacqualine K. Boog

ONE OF MY FAVORITES.

꧁꧂

As one who likes to have all her "ducks" in a row I truly
appreciate this one. (Geese will work in a pinch!)

Jacqualine K. Boog

OLD MACKINAC POINT LIGHTHOUSE WITH THE MACKINAW BRIDGE.

⸎

ANOTHER OF MY FAVORITES AS THE SUN BREAKS THROUGH
THE CLOUDS OVER THE MIGHTY MAC.

Jacqualine K. Boog

SOMETIMES A SINGLE TREE SPEAKS MORE THAN THE ENTIRE FOREST.
"....AND HAVING DONE ALL, TO STAND." EPH. 6:13